FERRET
COLORING BOOK

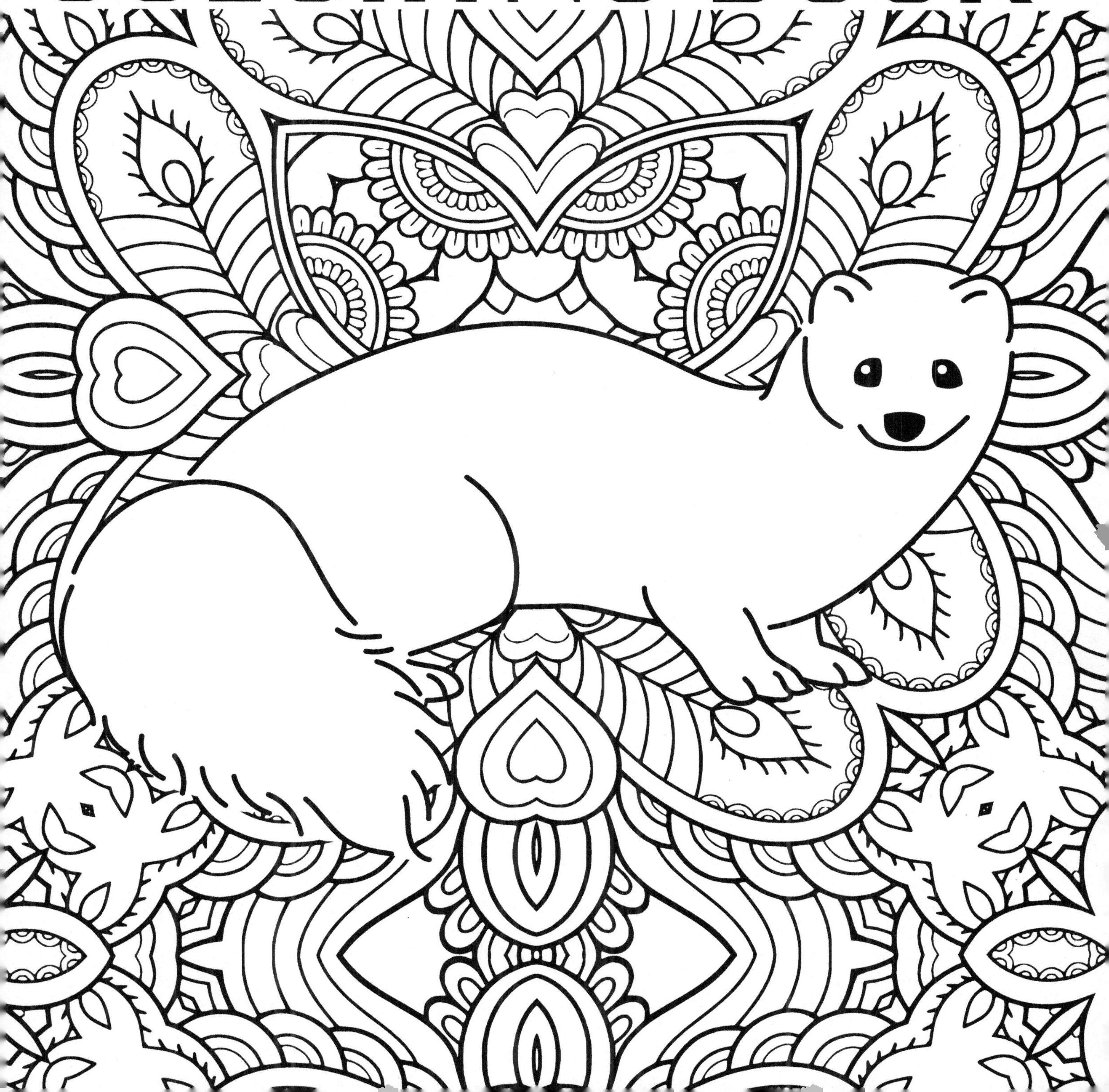

THIS BOOK BELONGS TO:

COLOR TEST PAGE

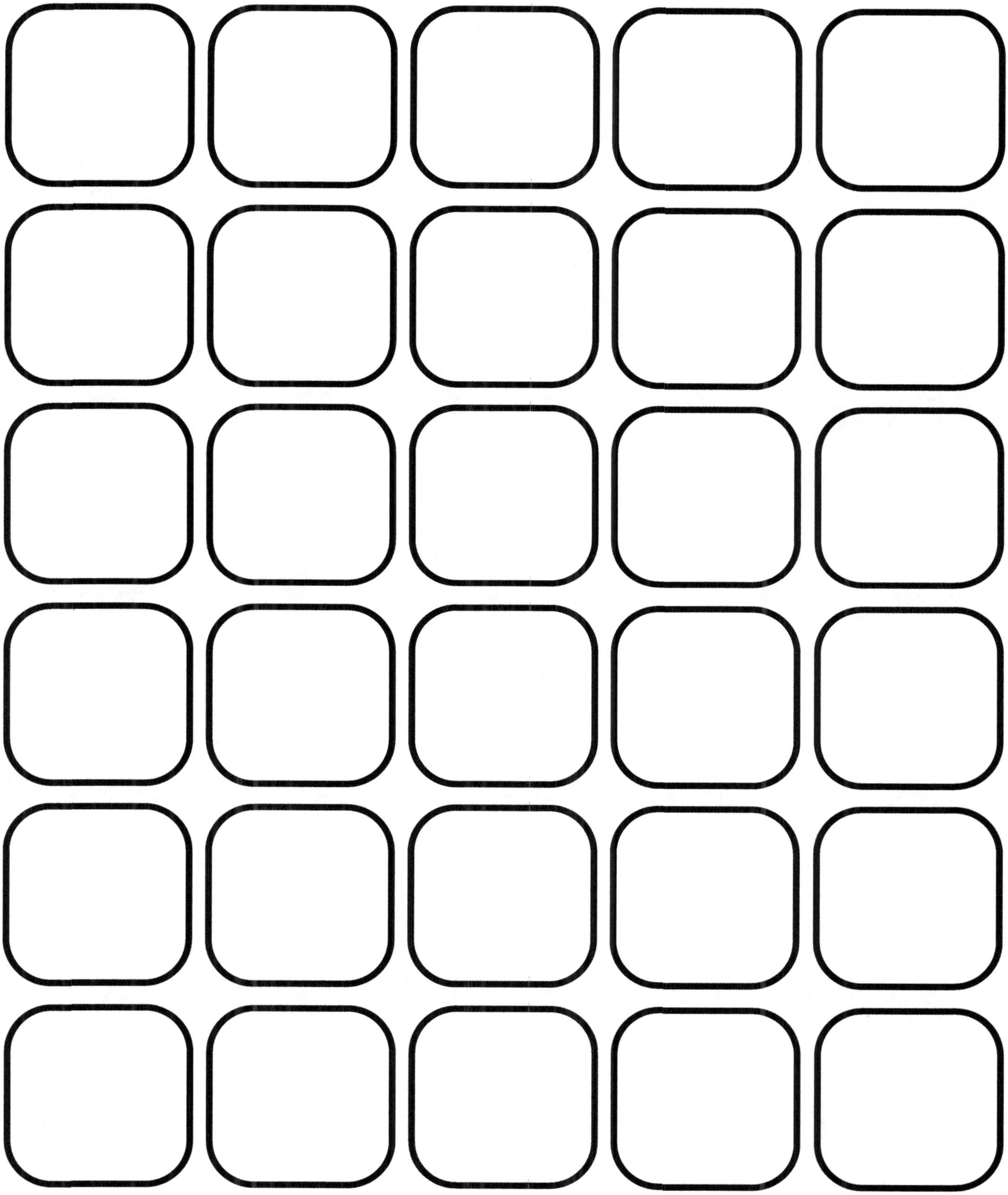

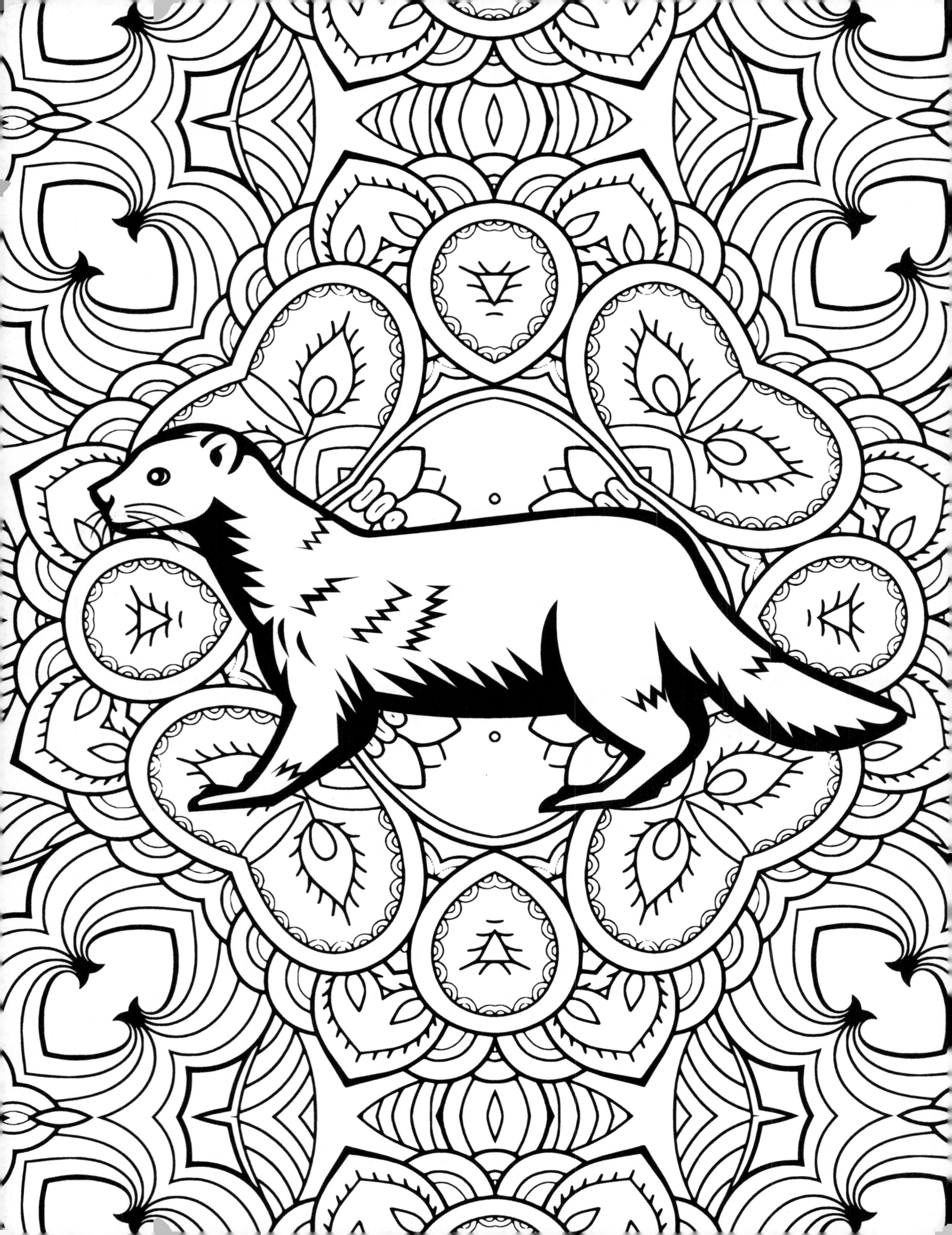

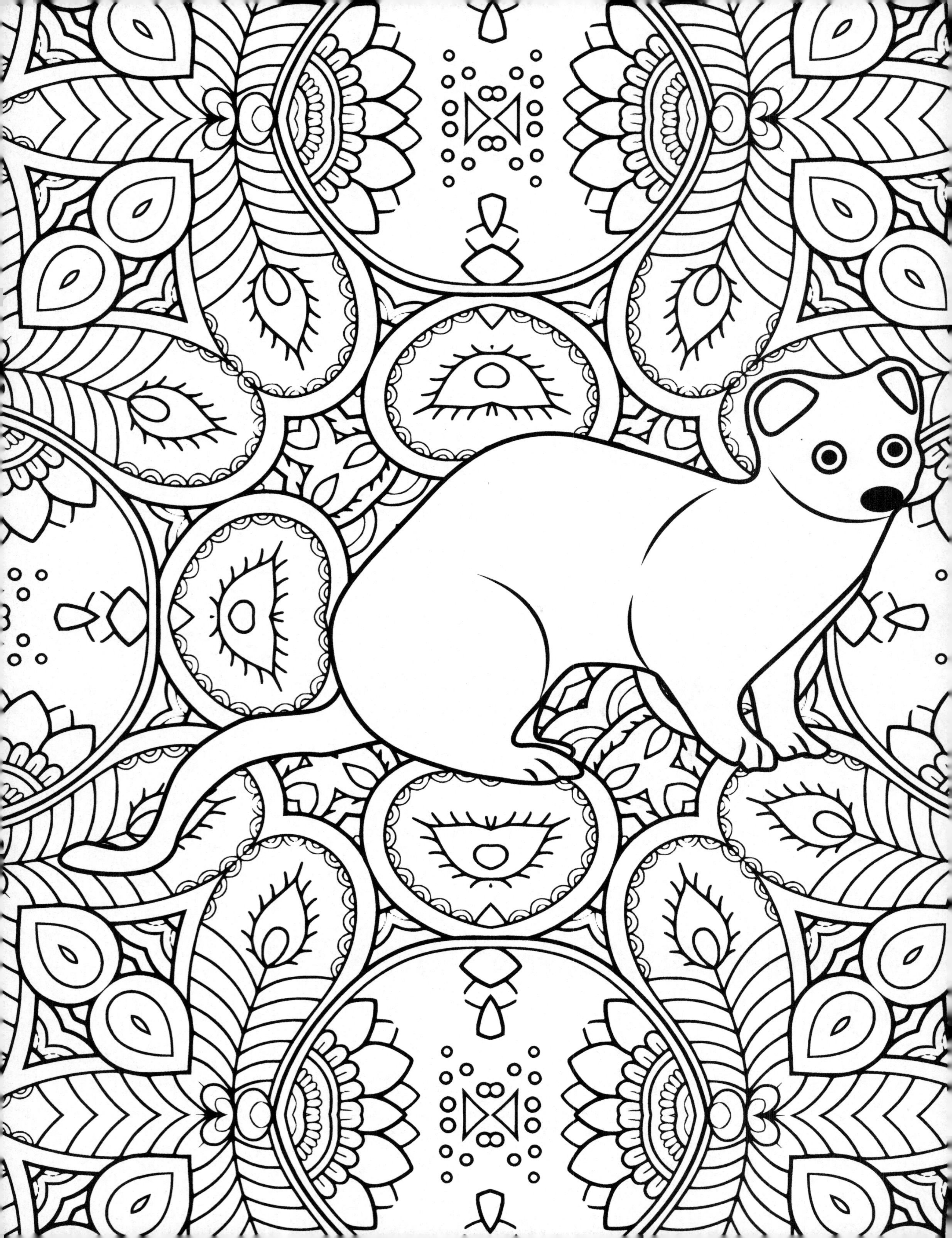

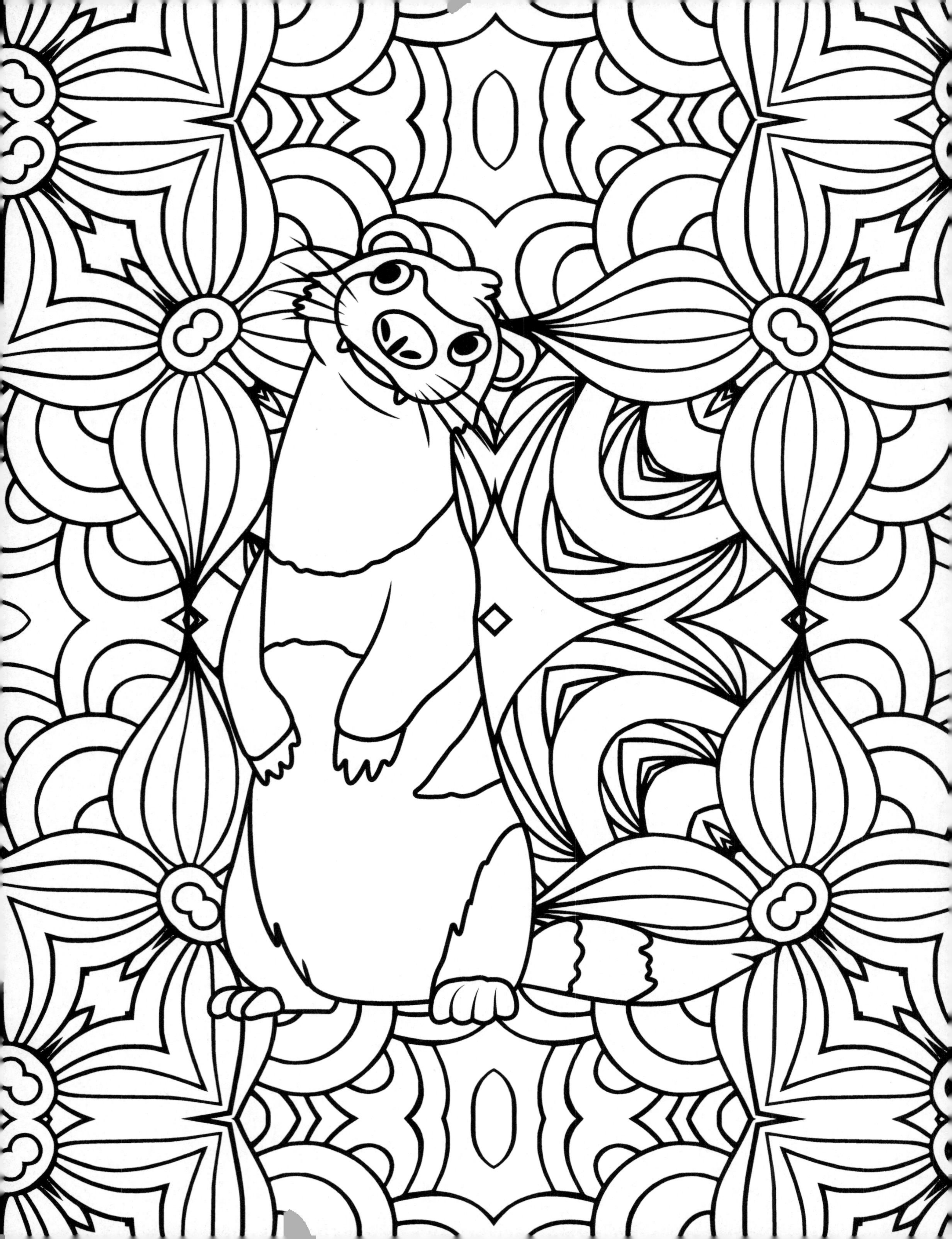

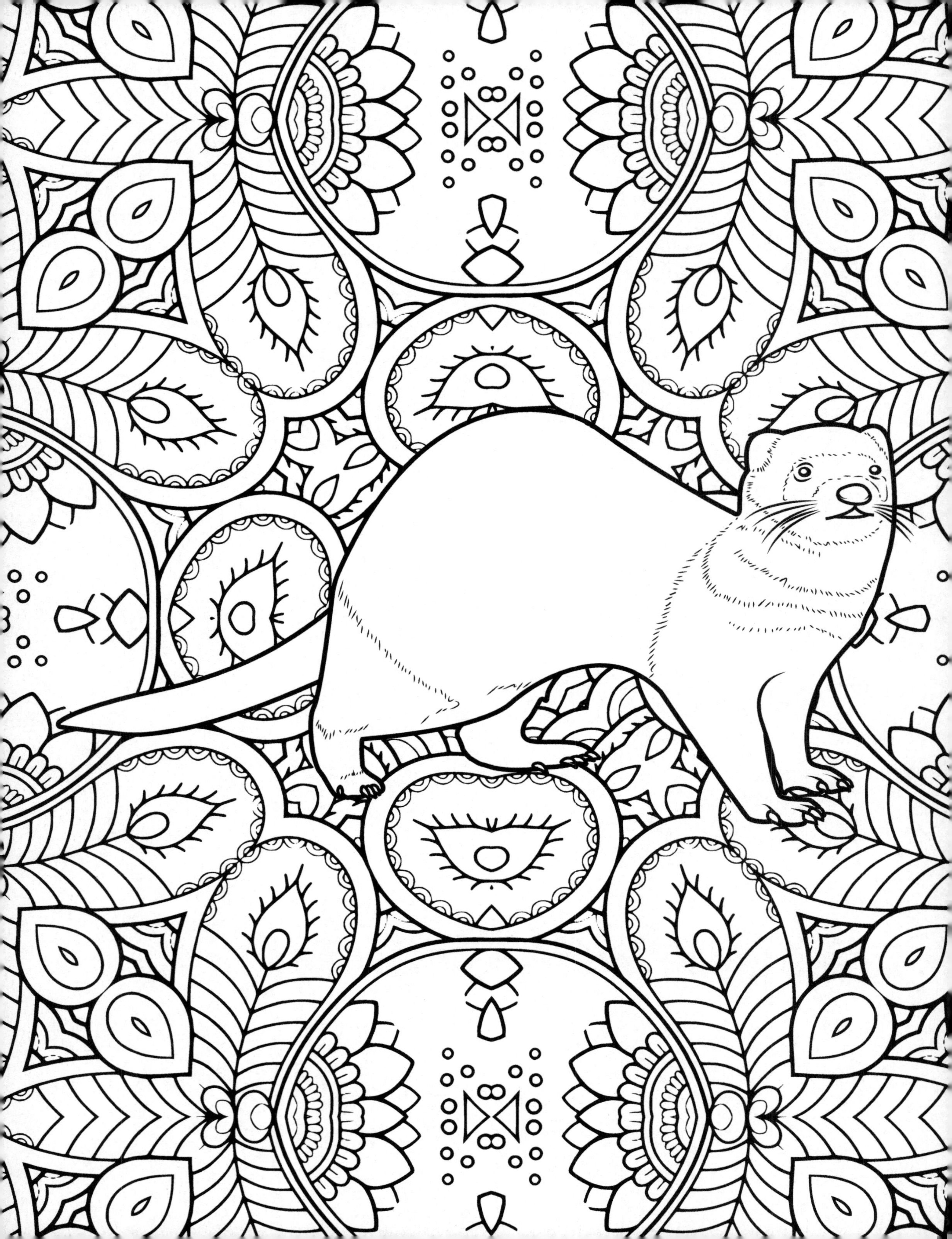

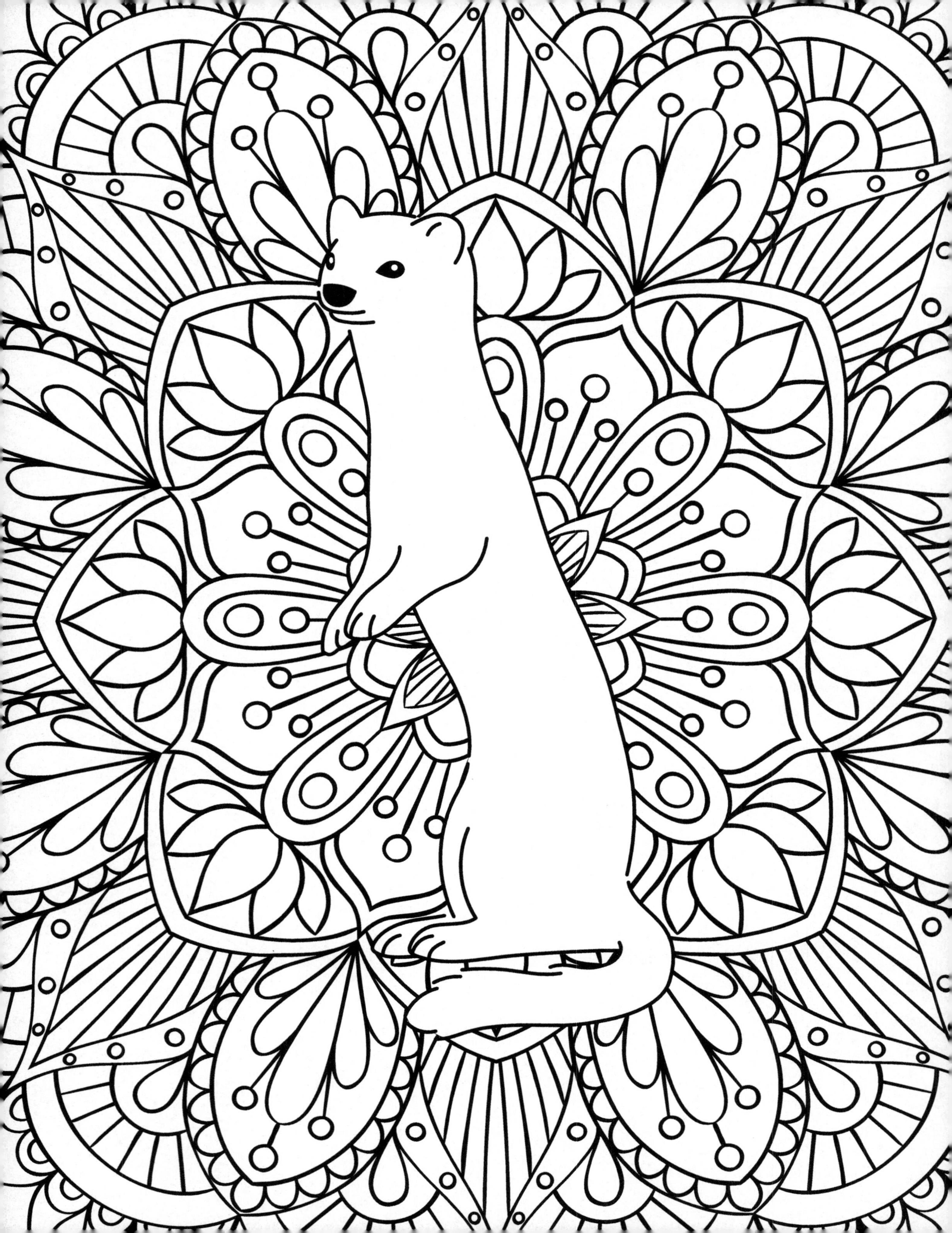

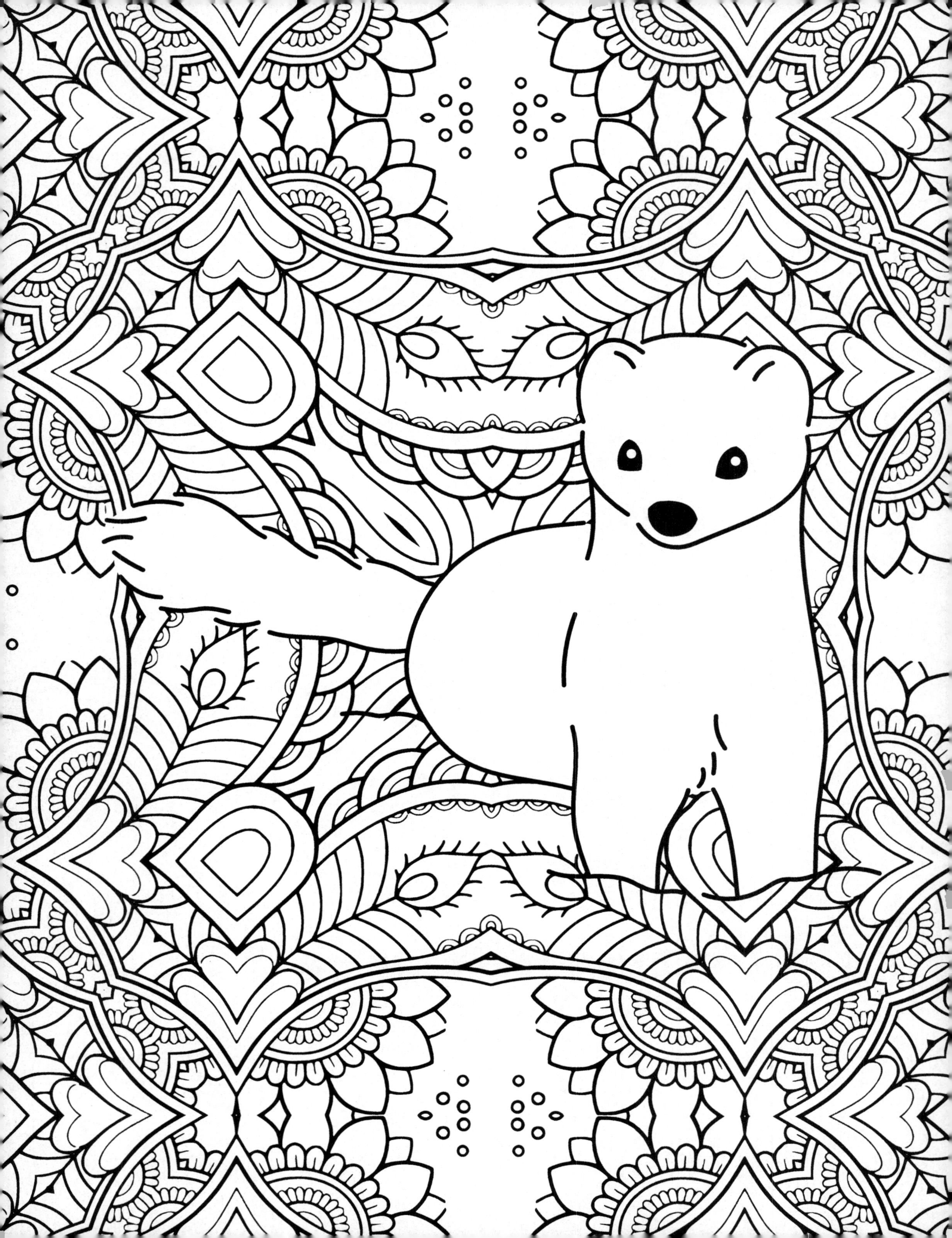

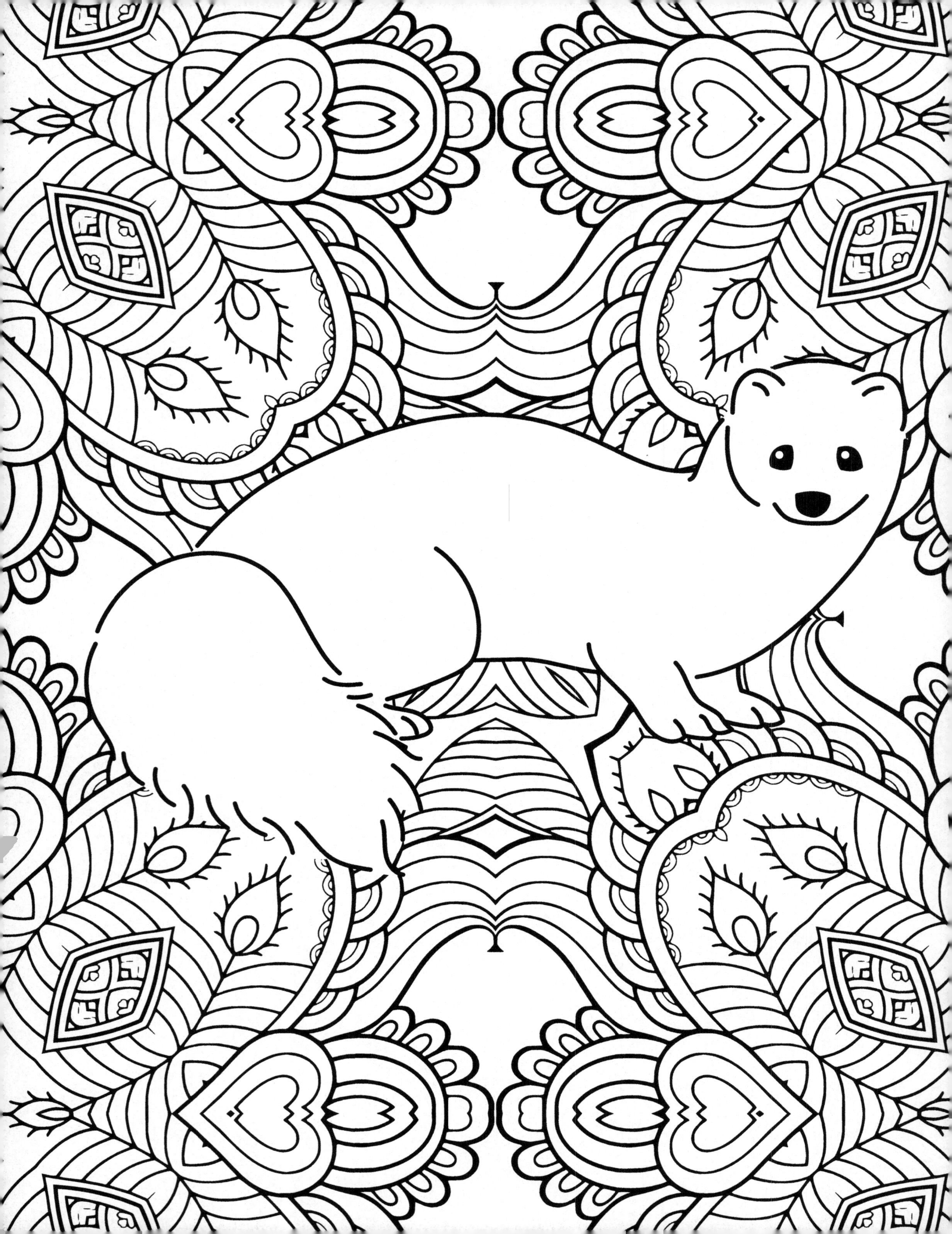

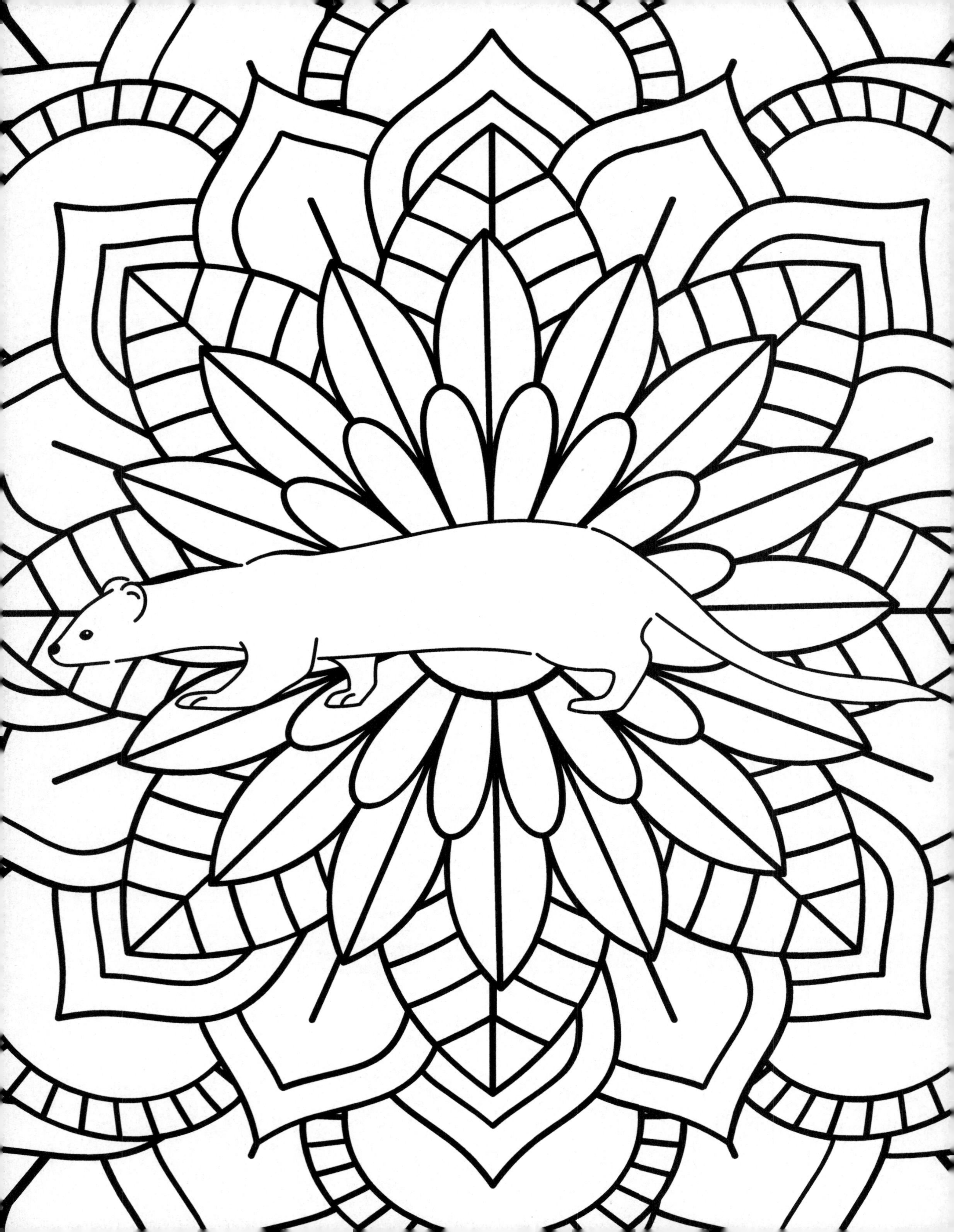

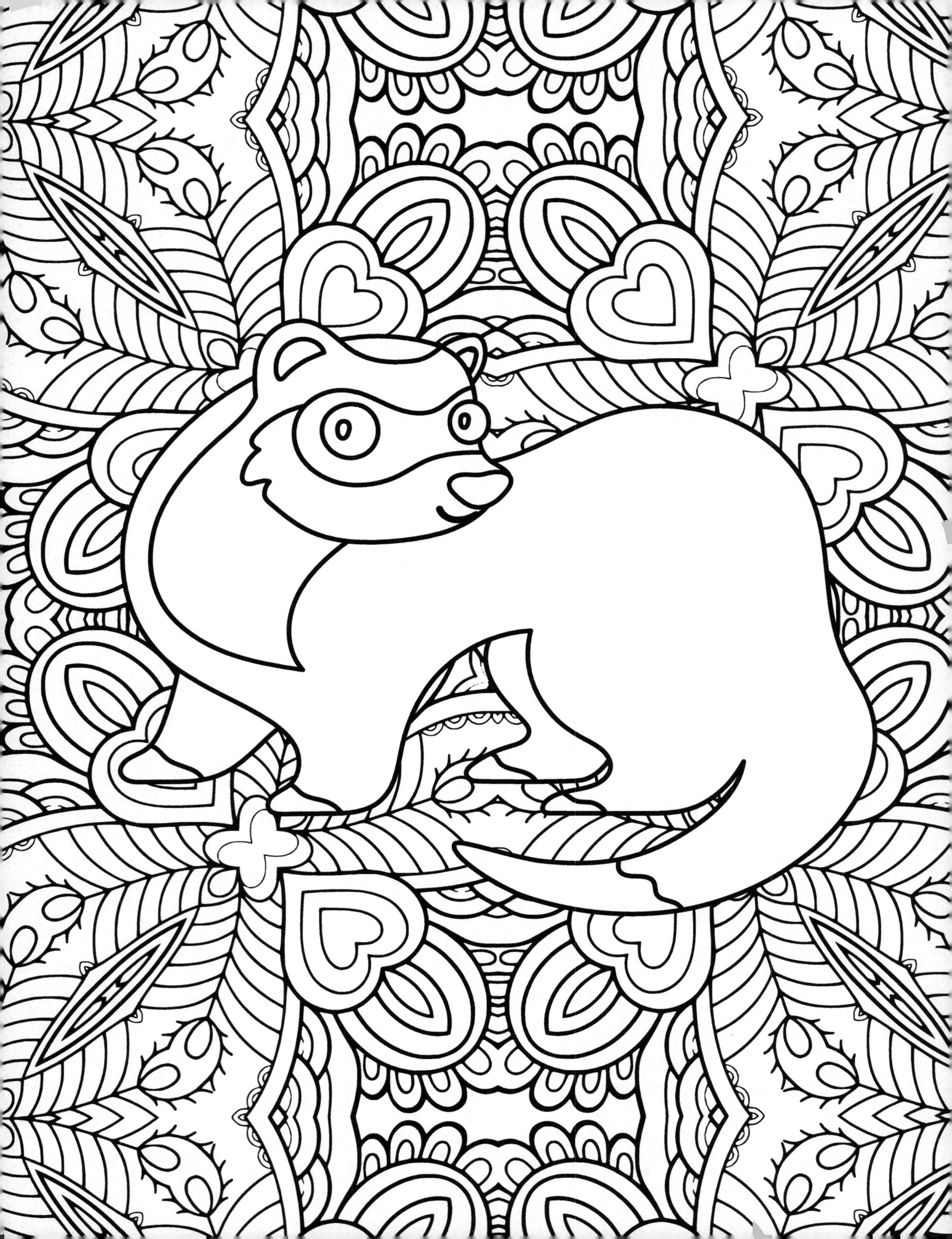

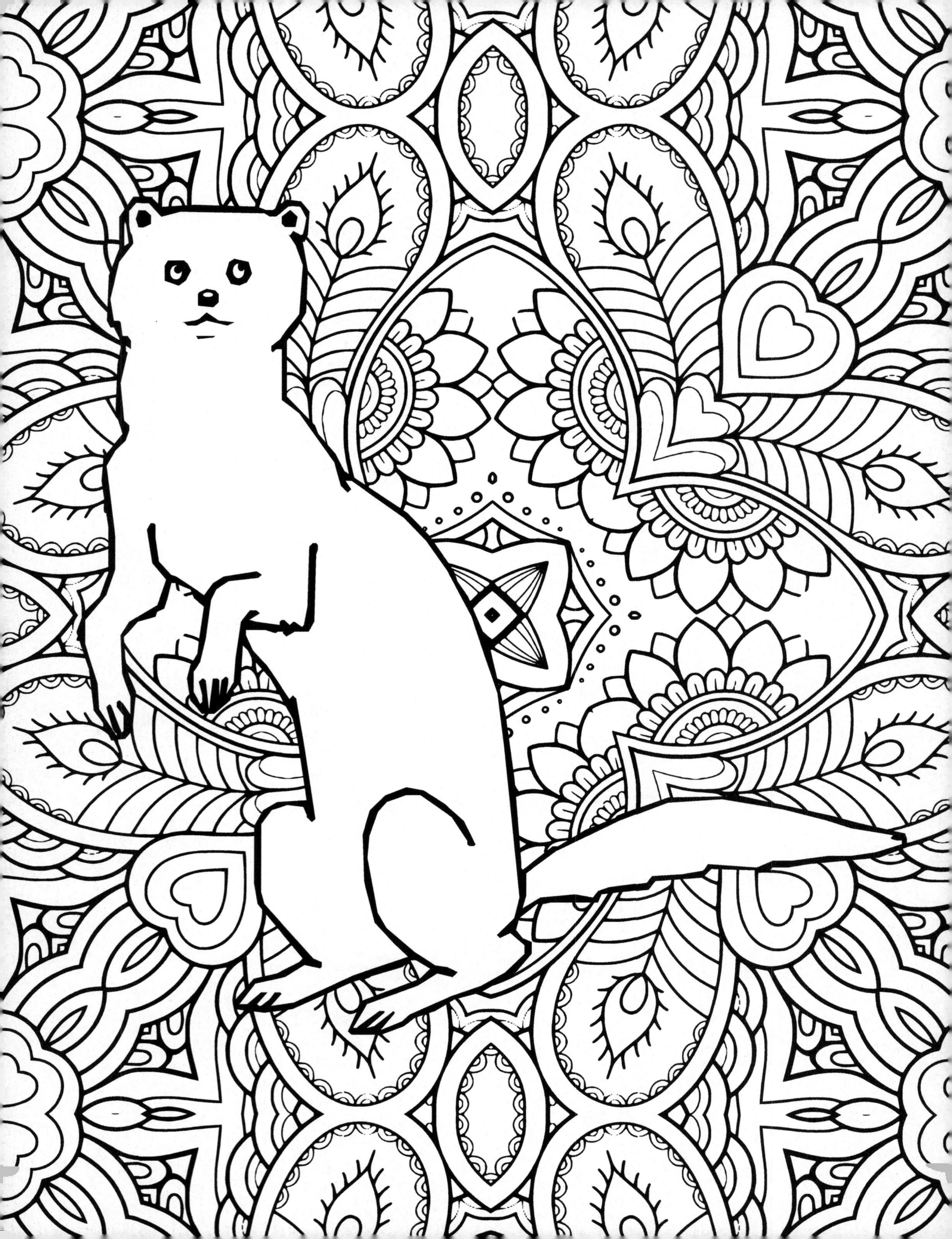

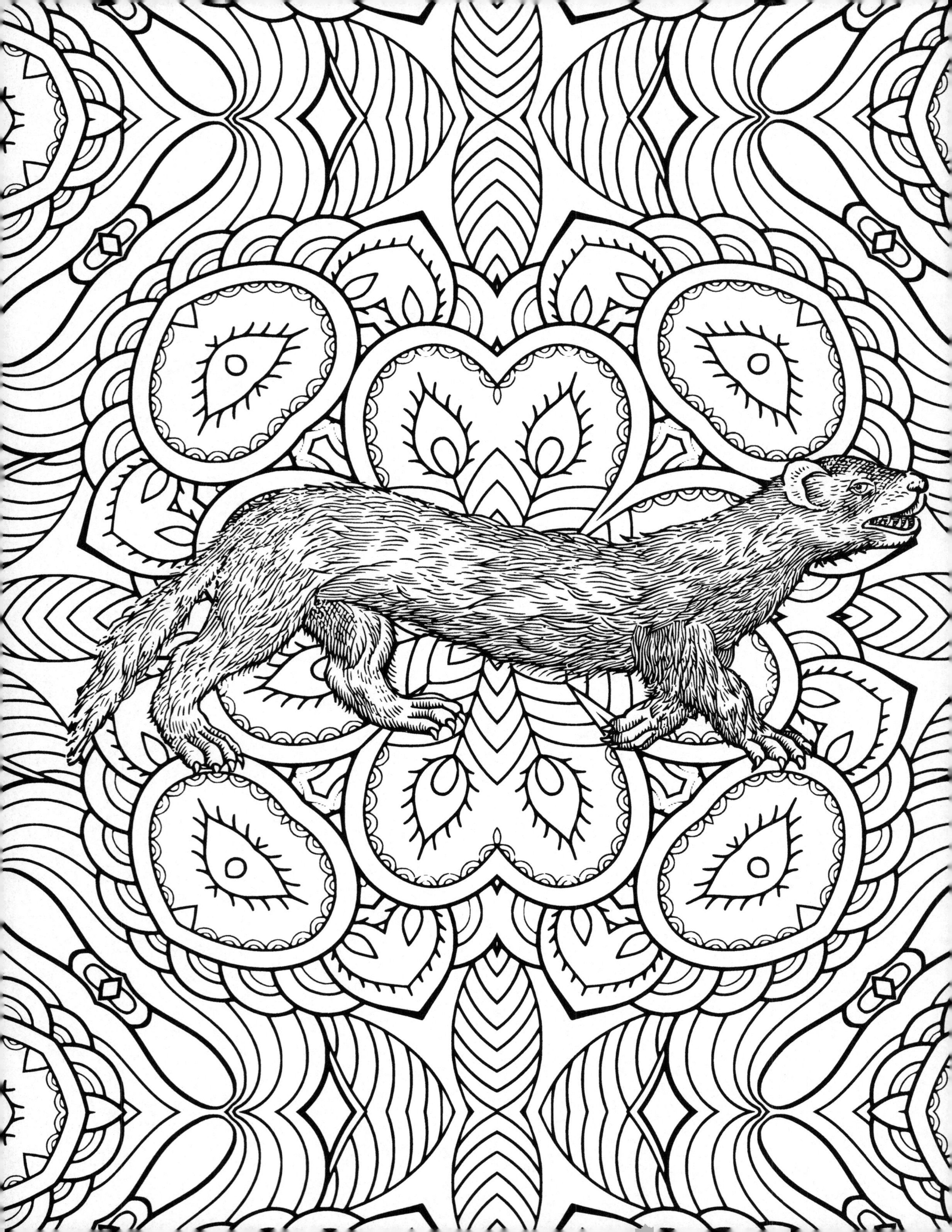

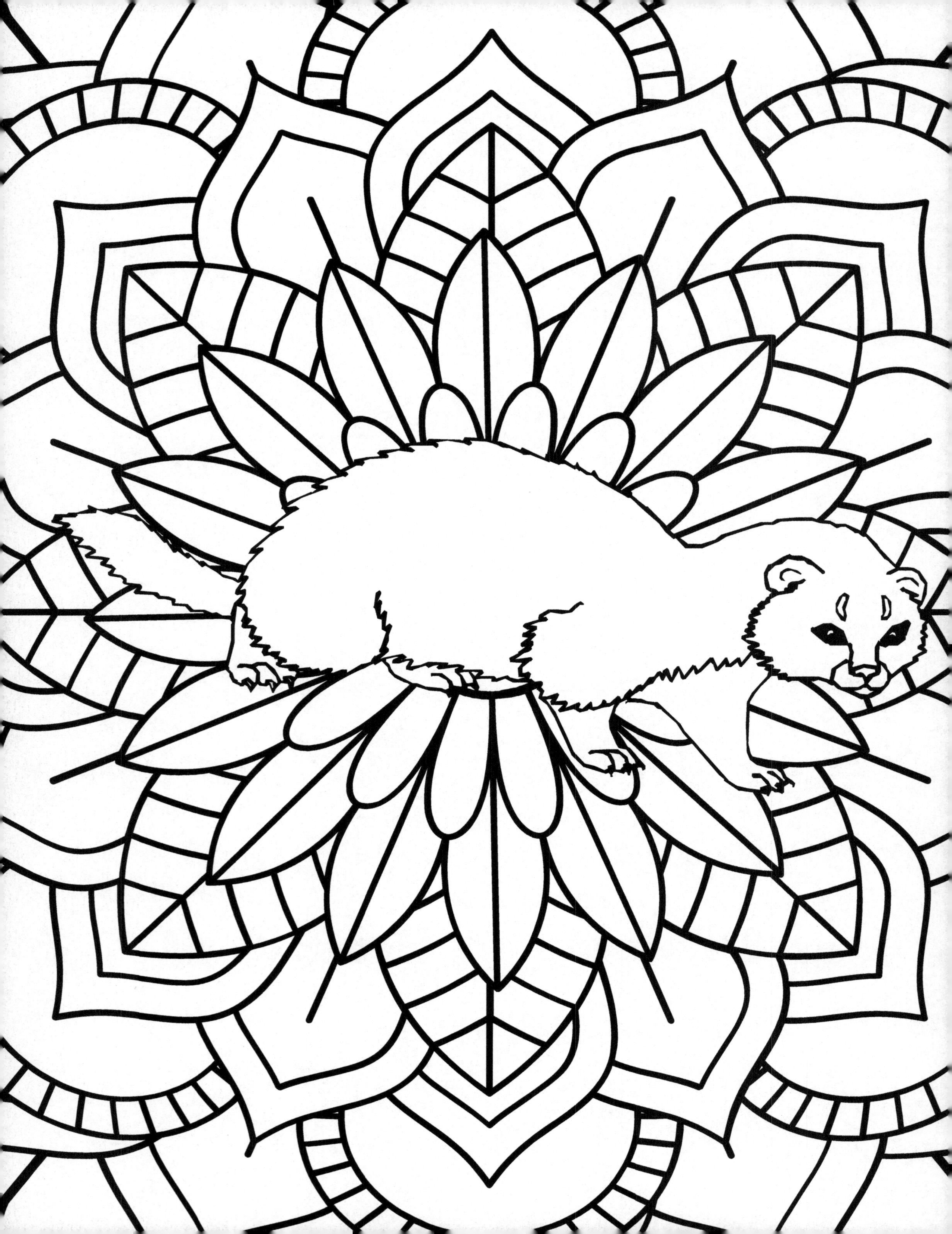

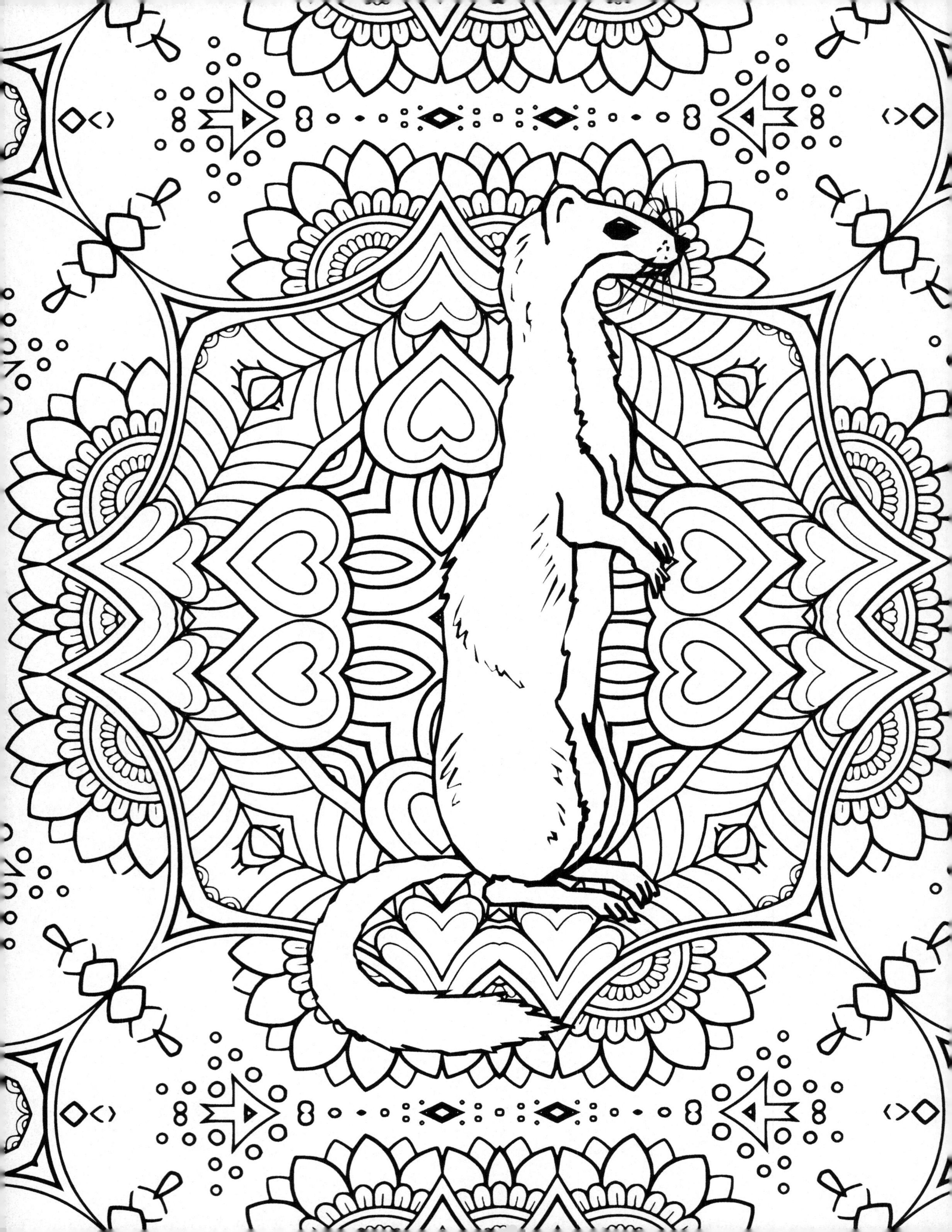

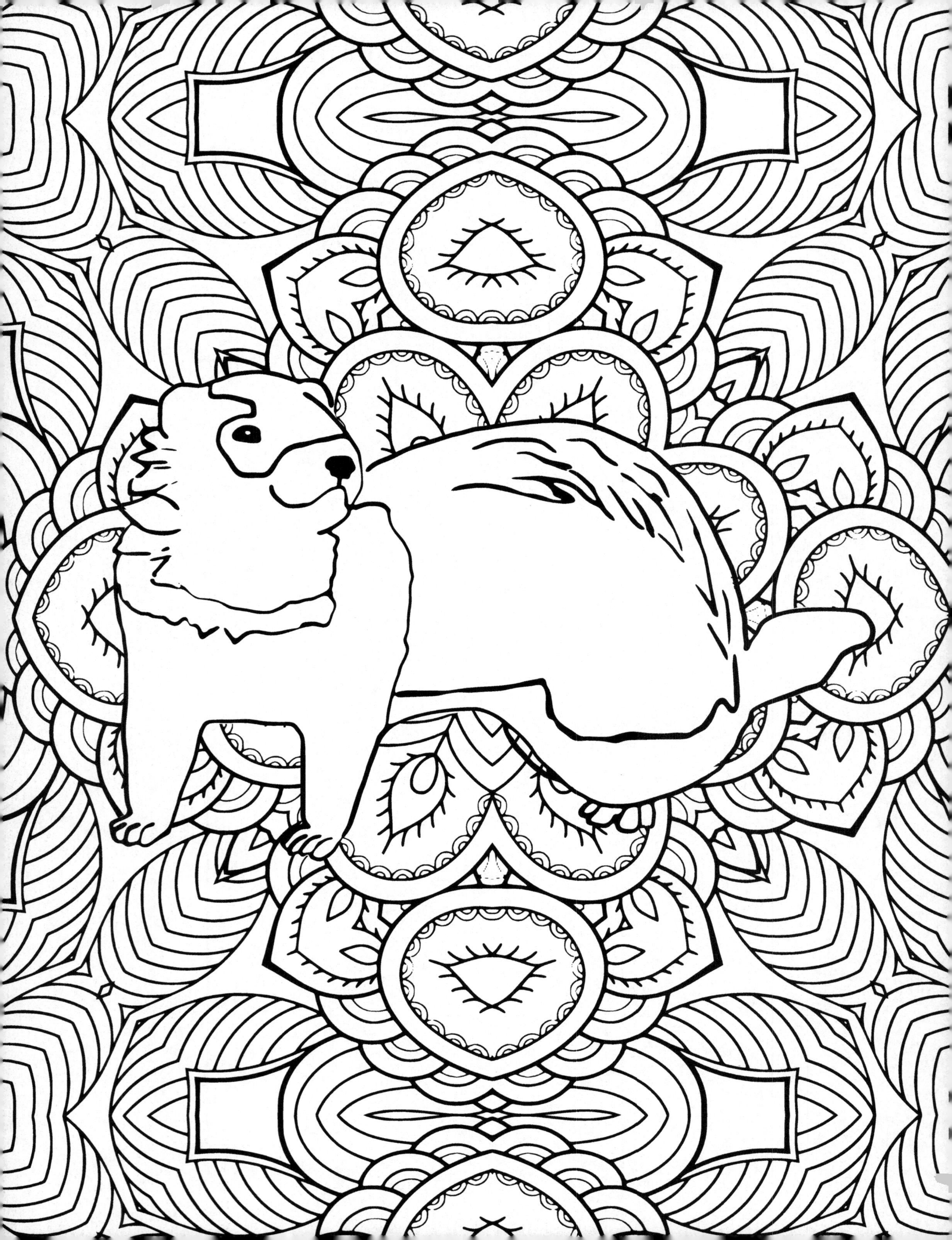

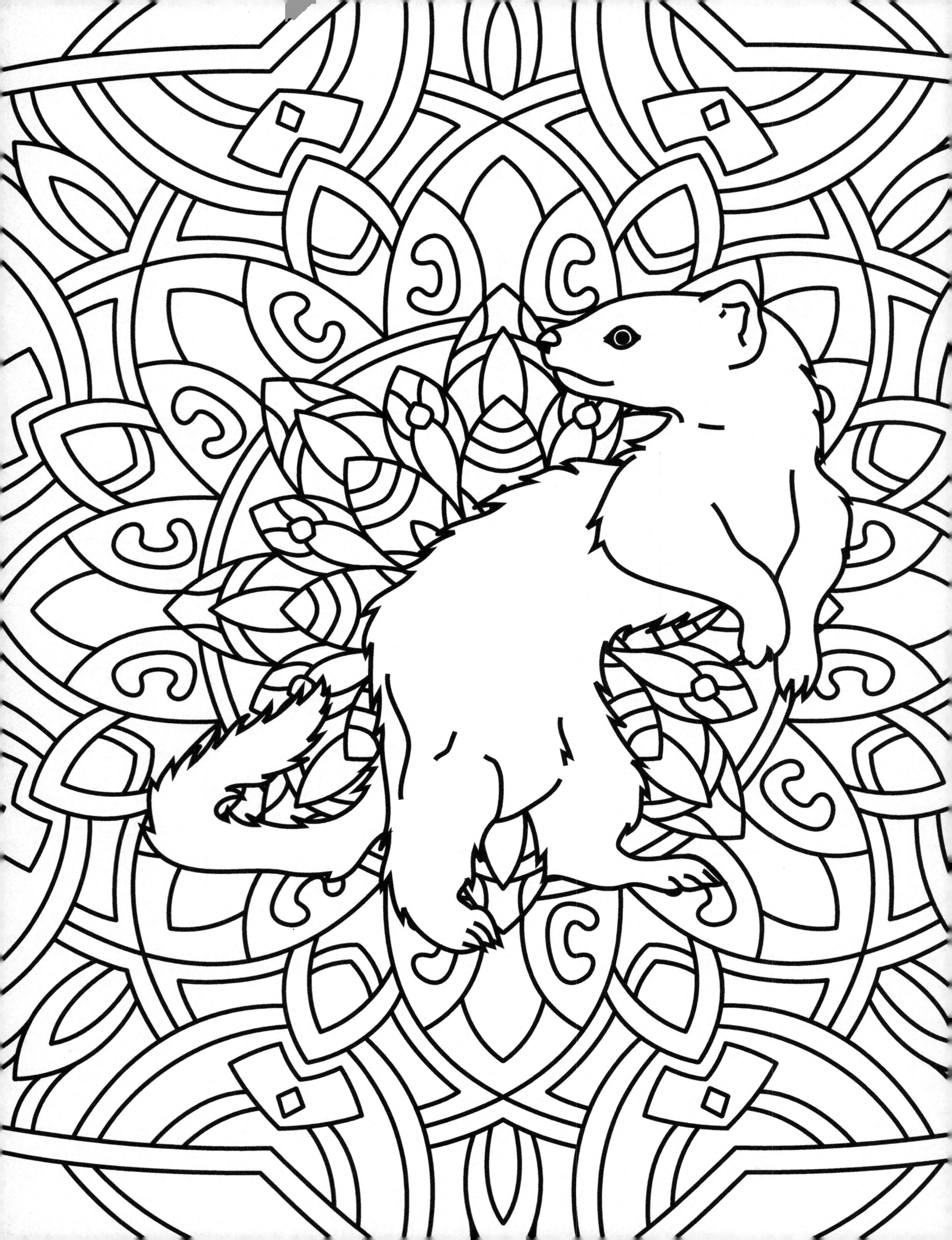

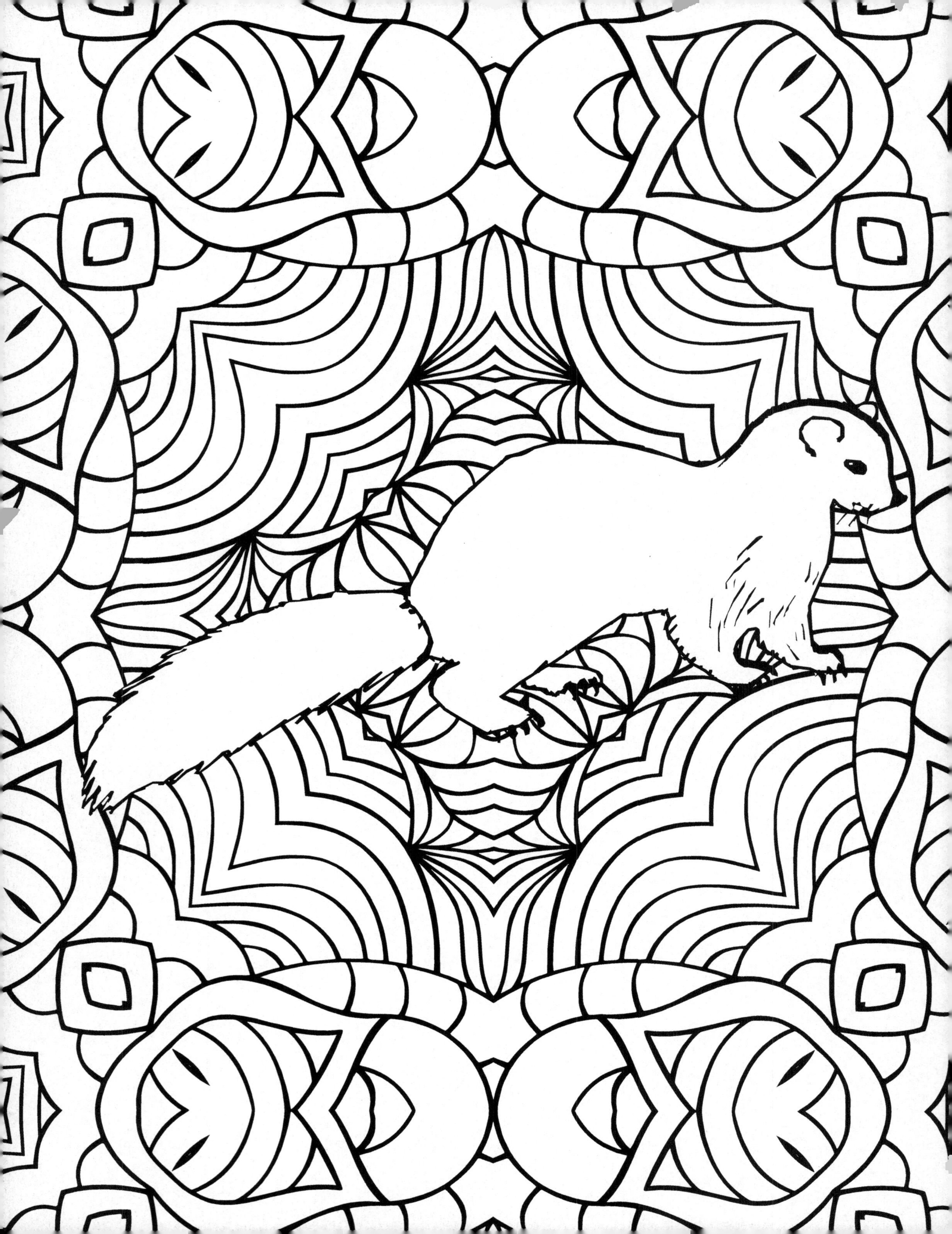

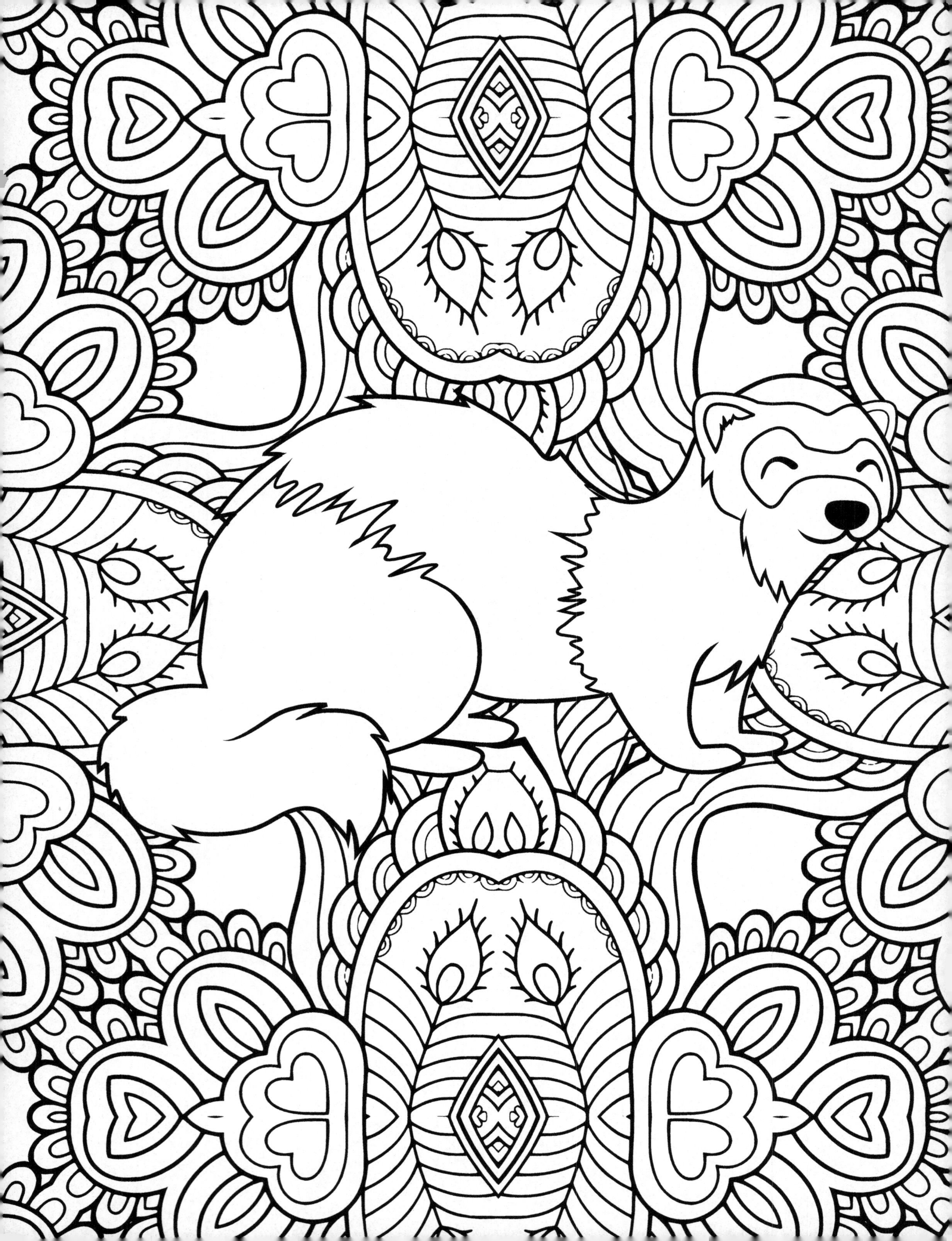

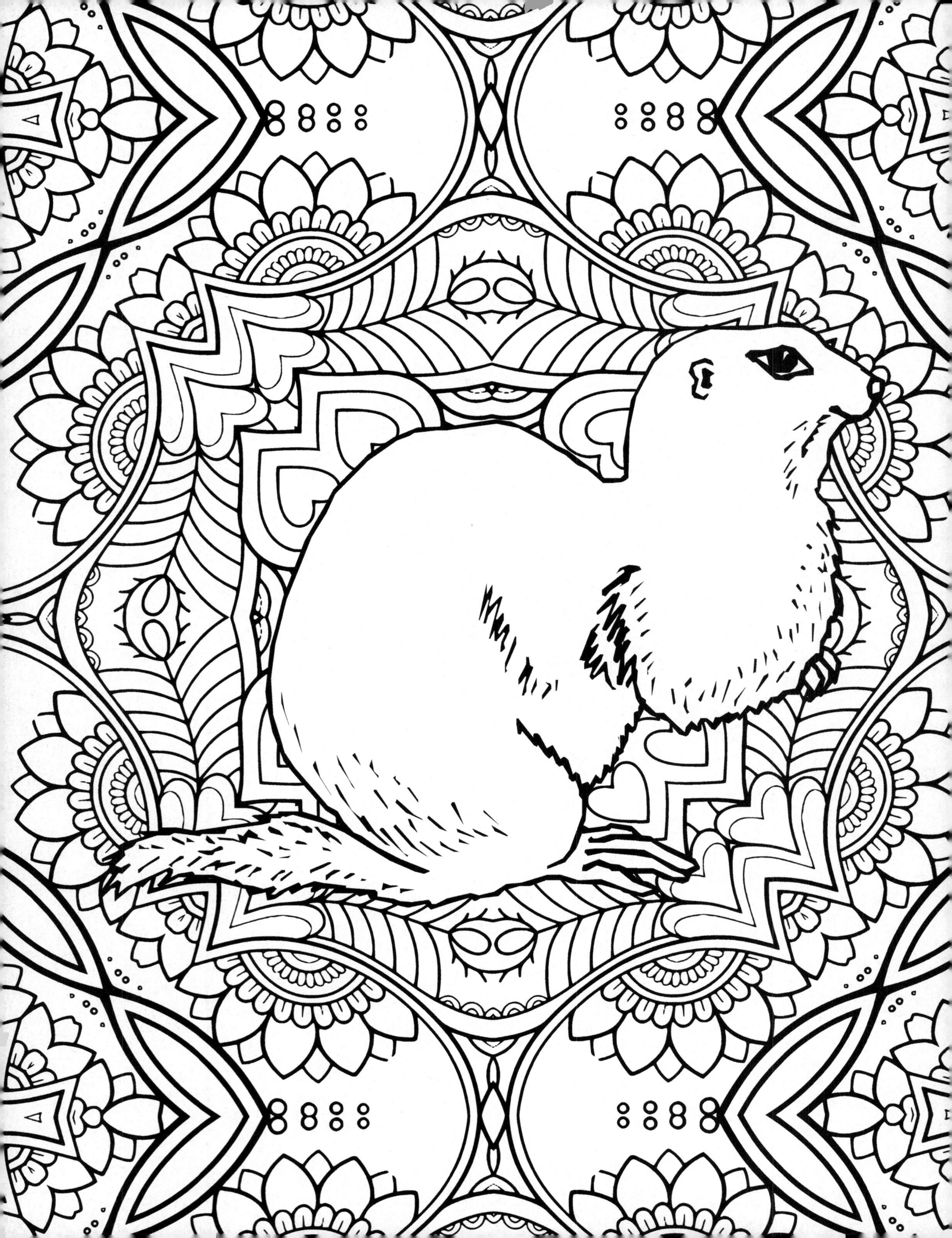

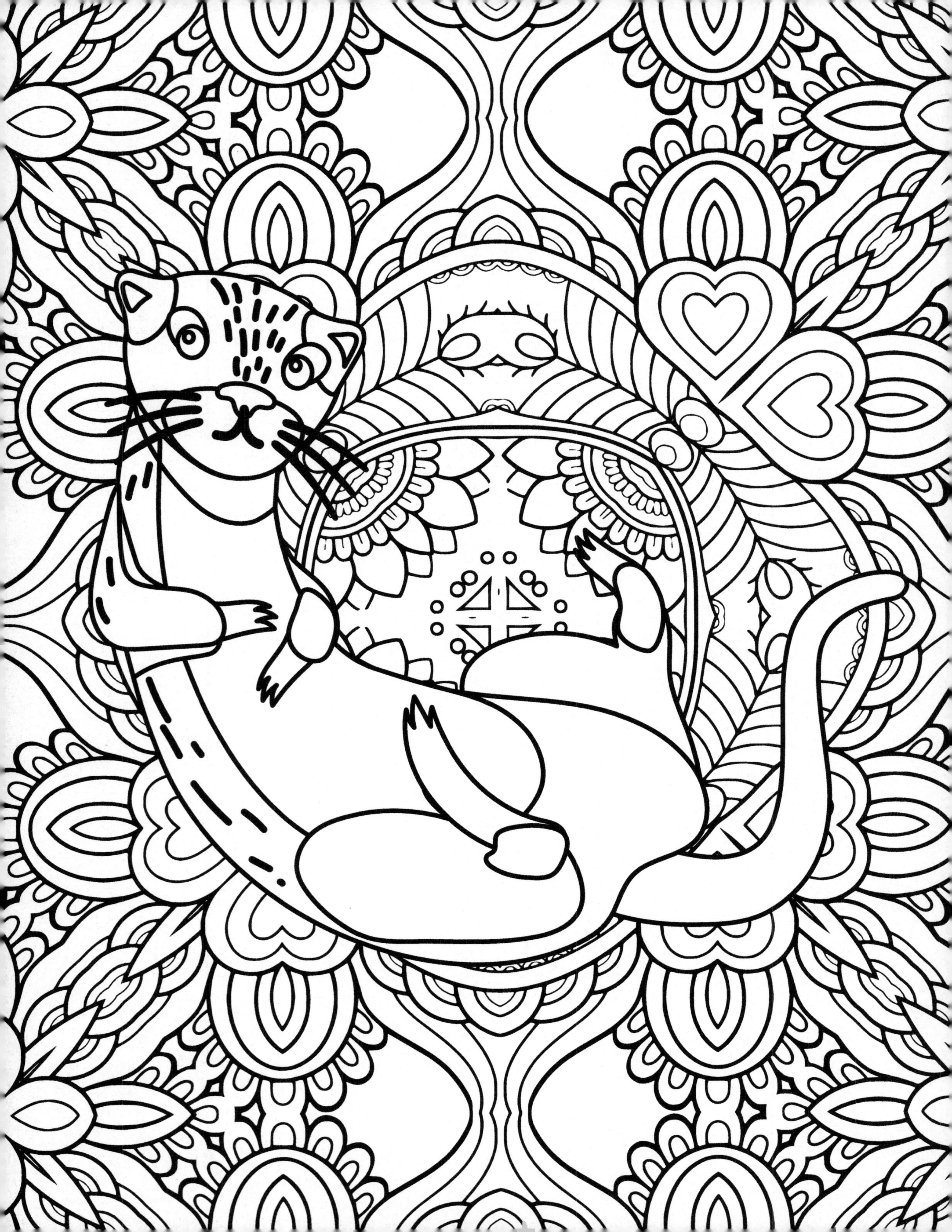

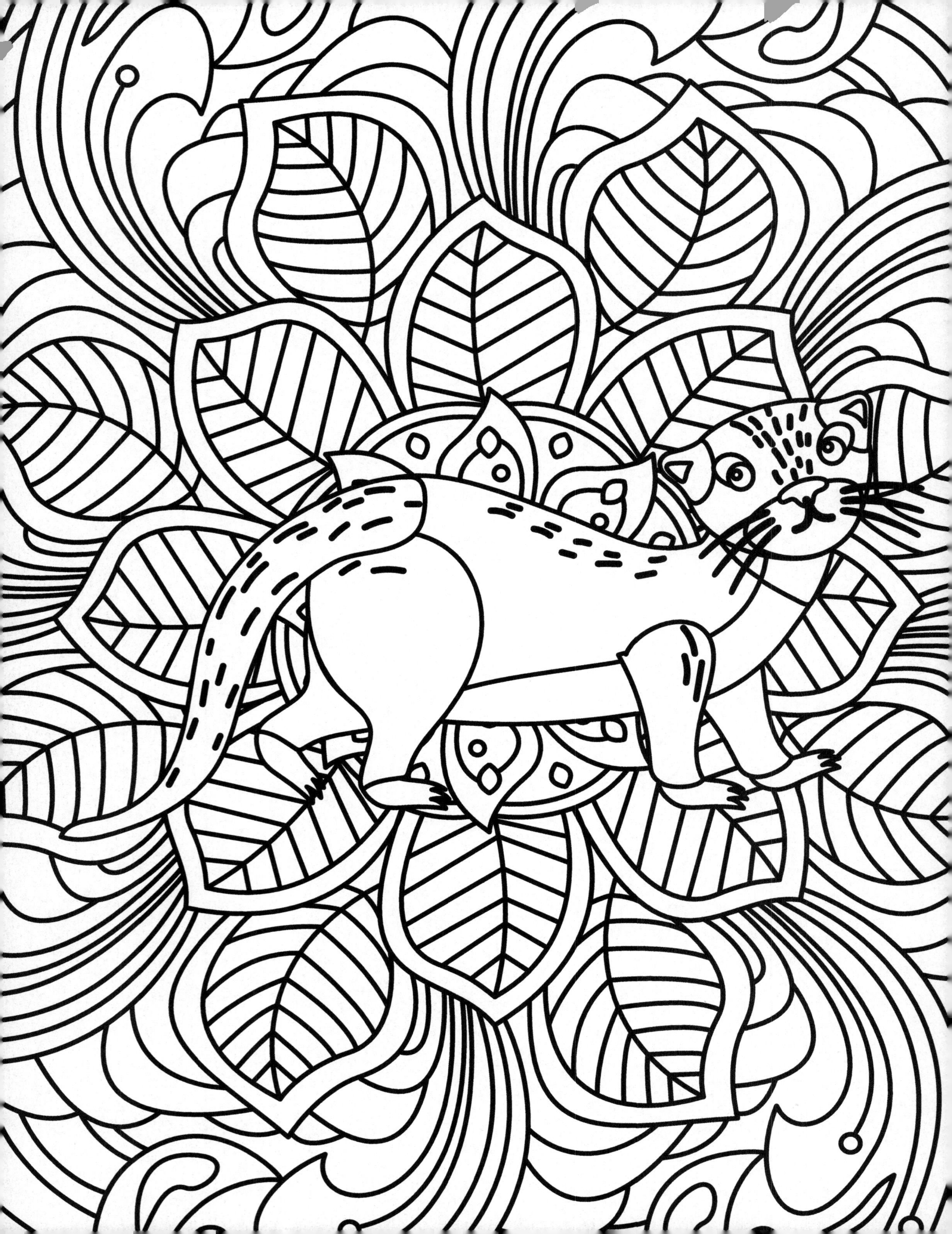

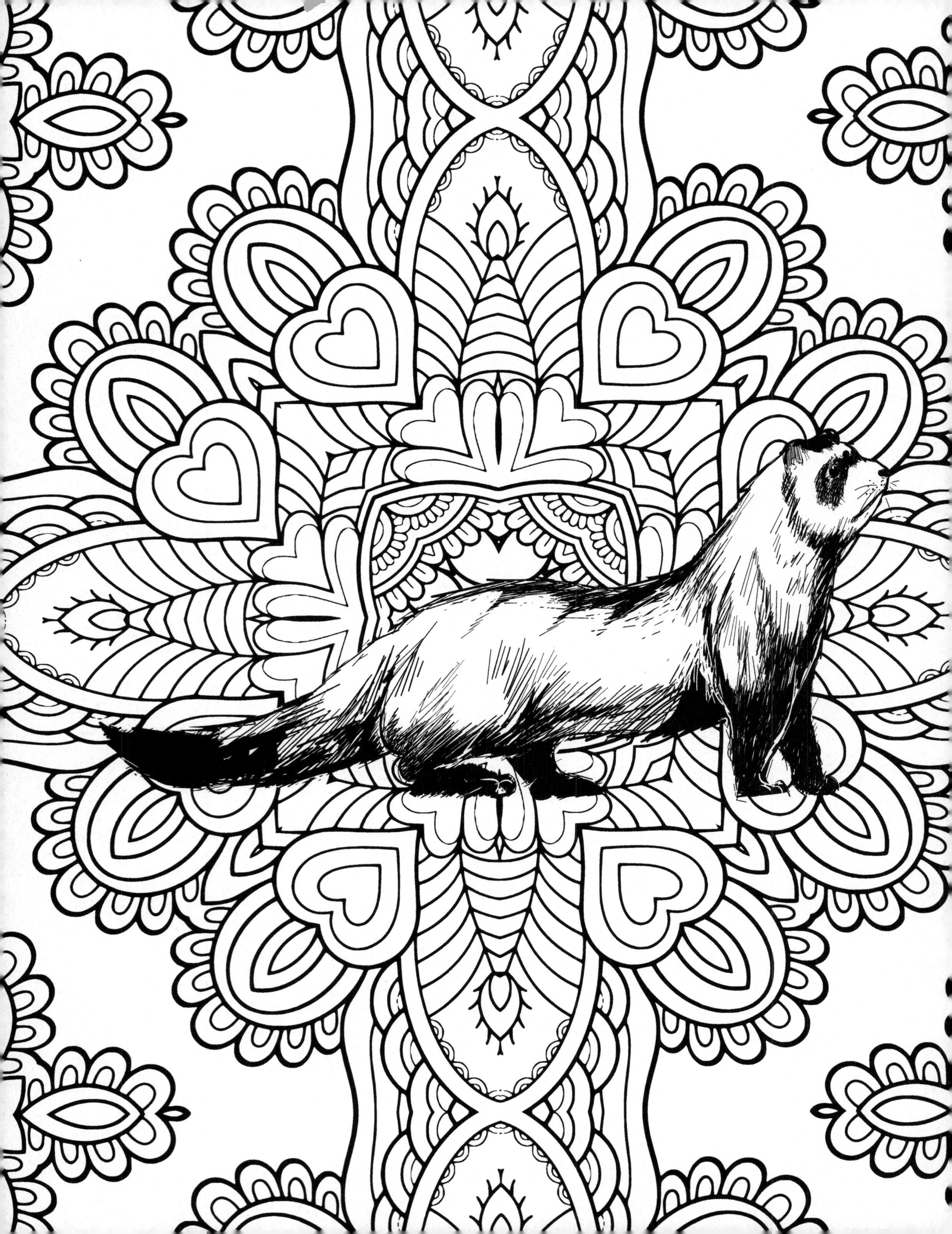

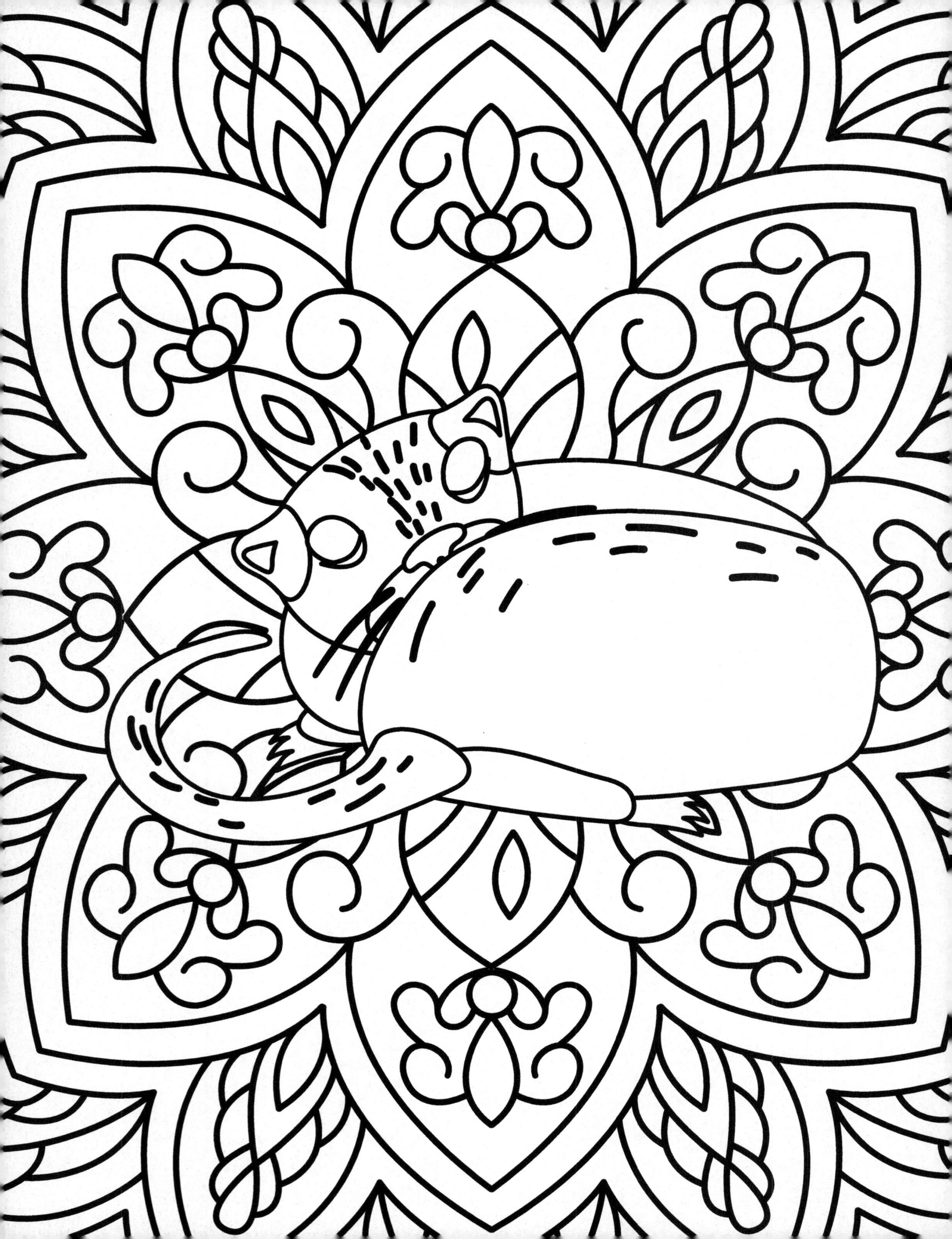

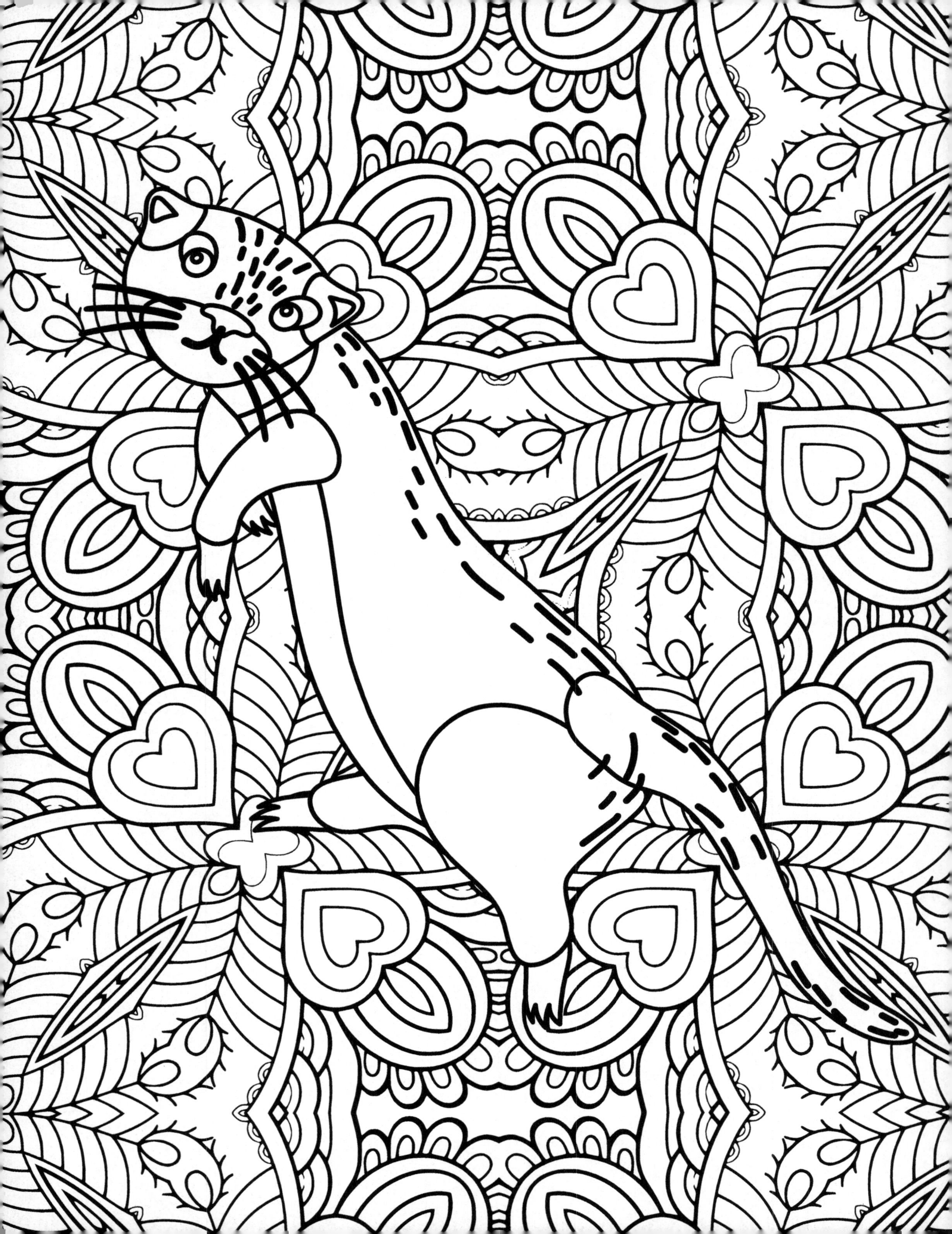

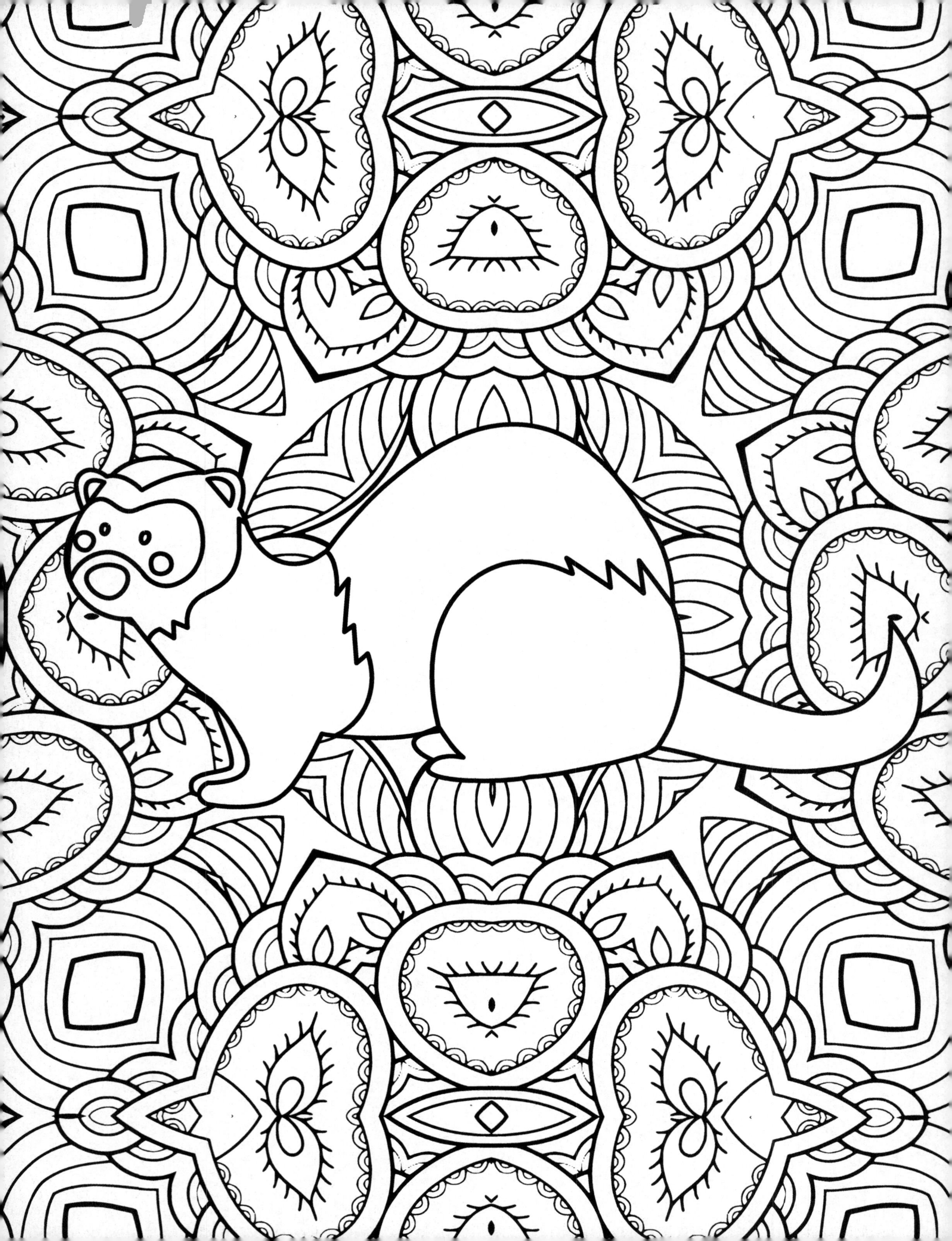

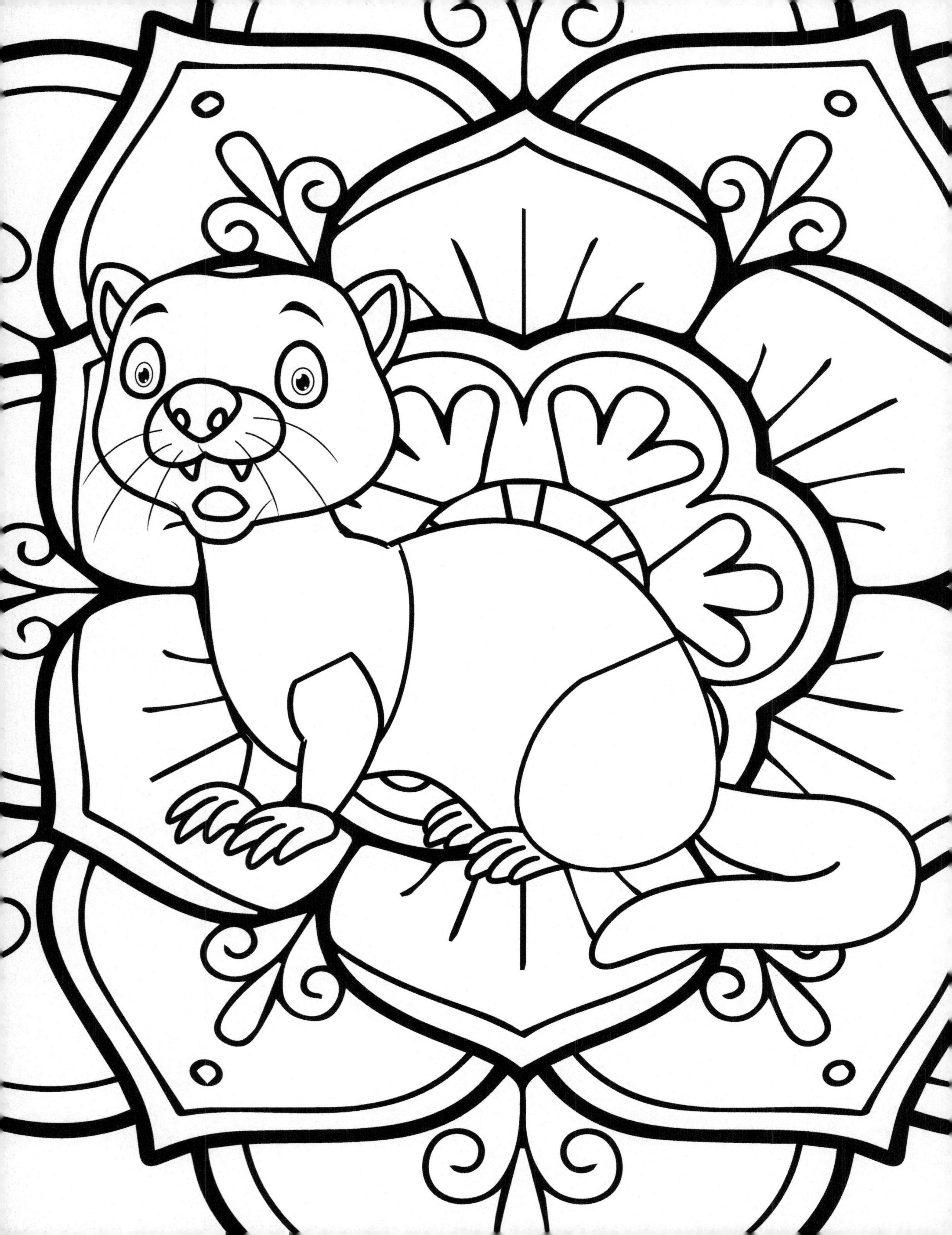

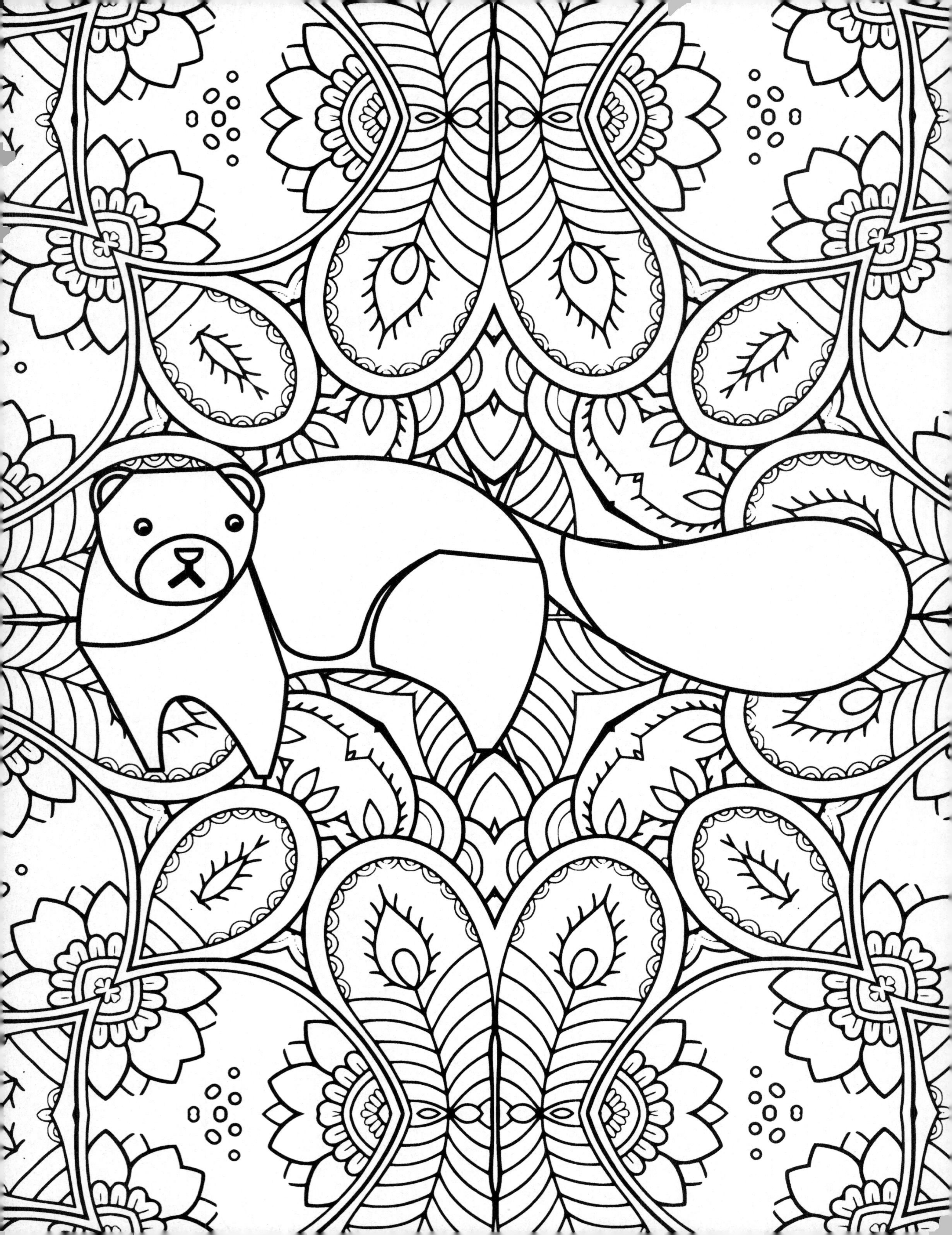

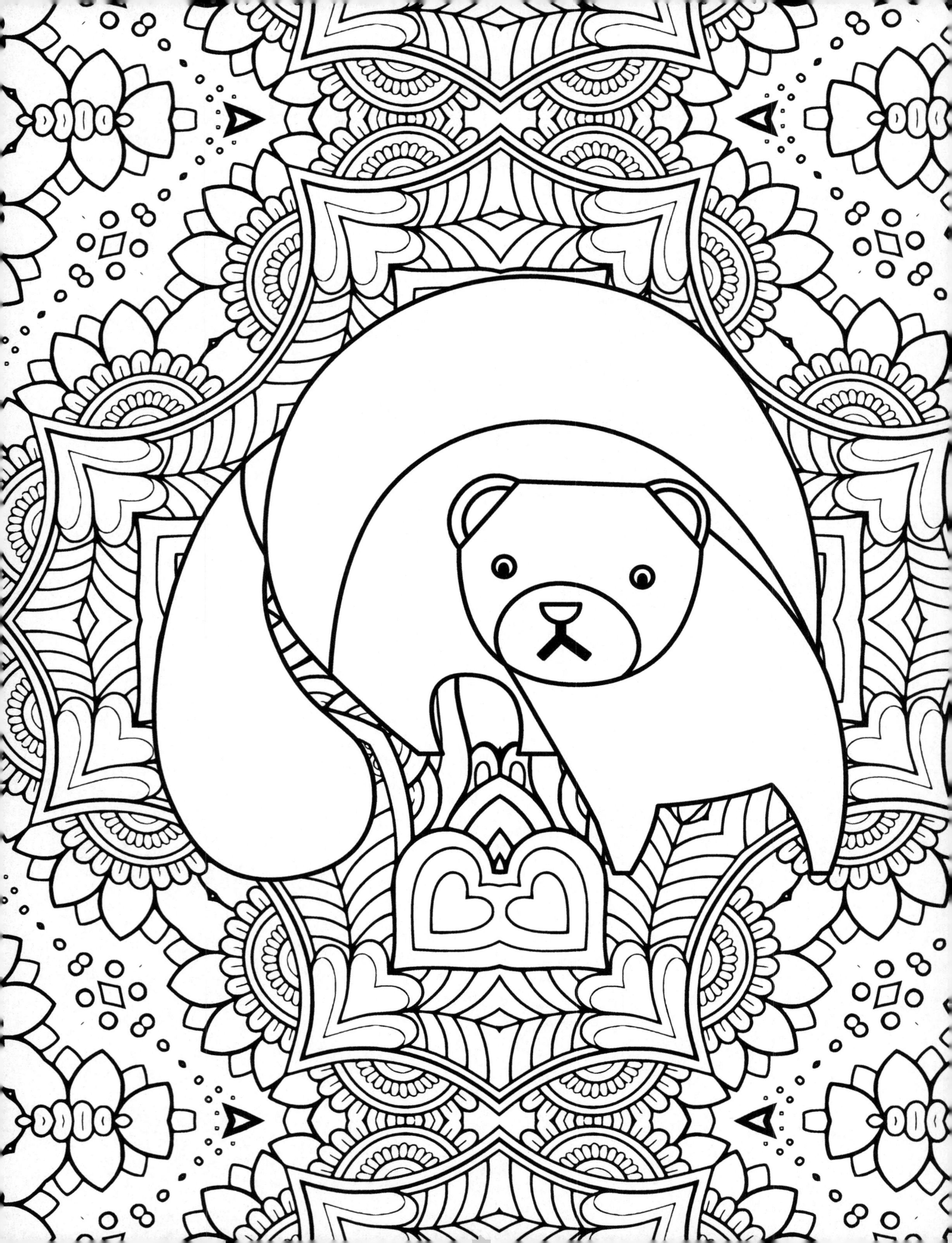

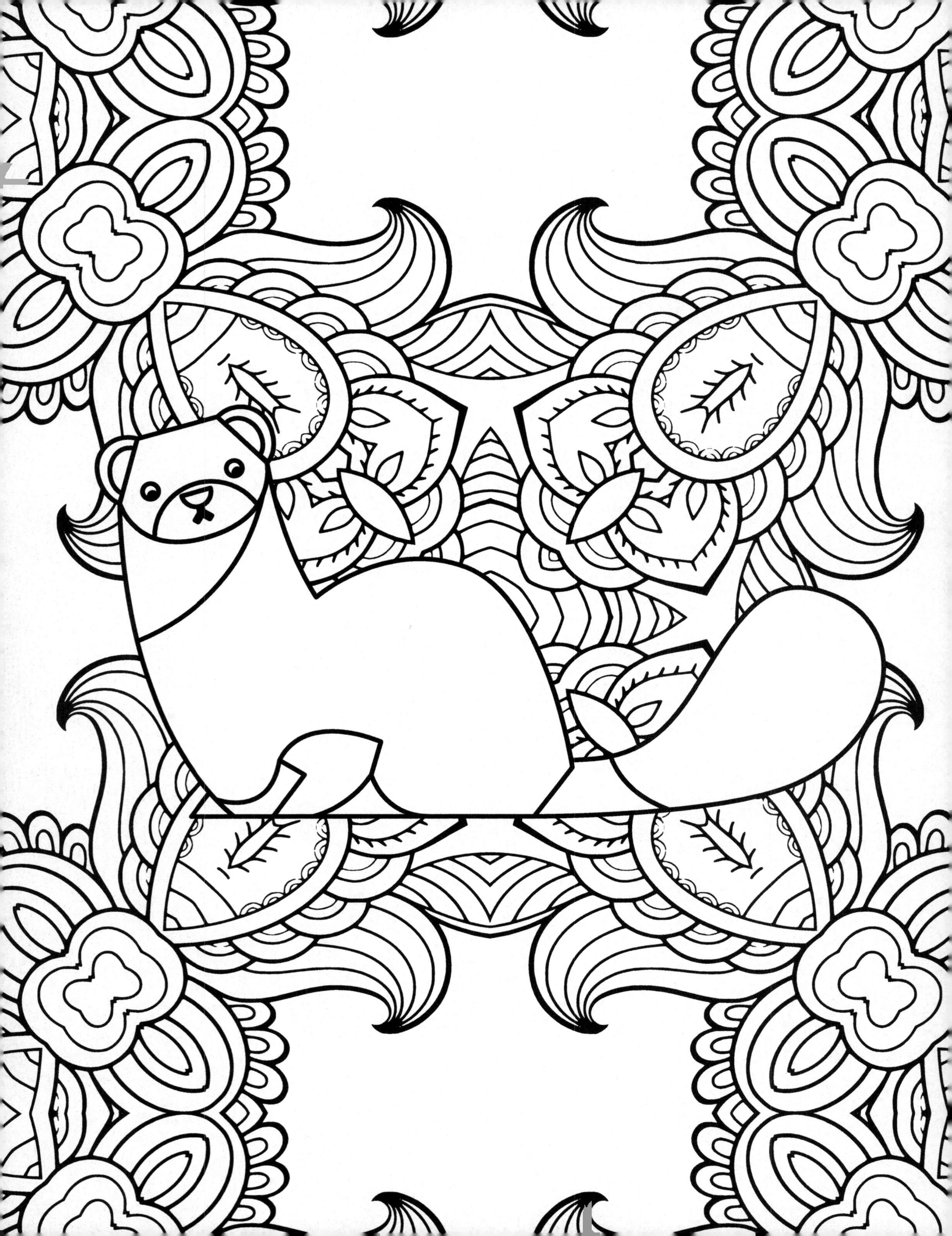

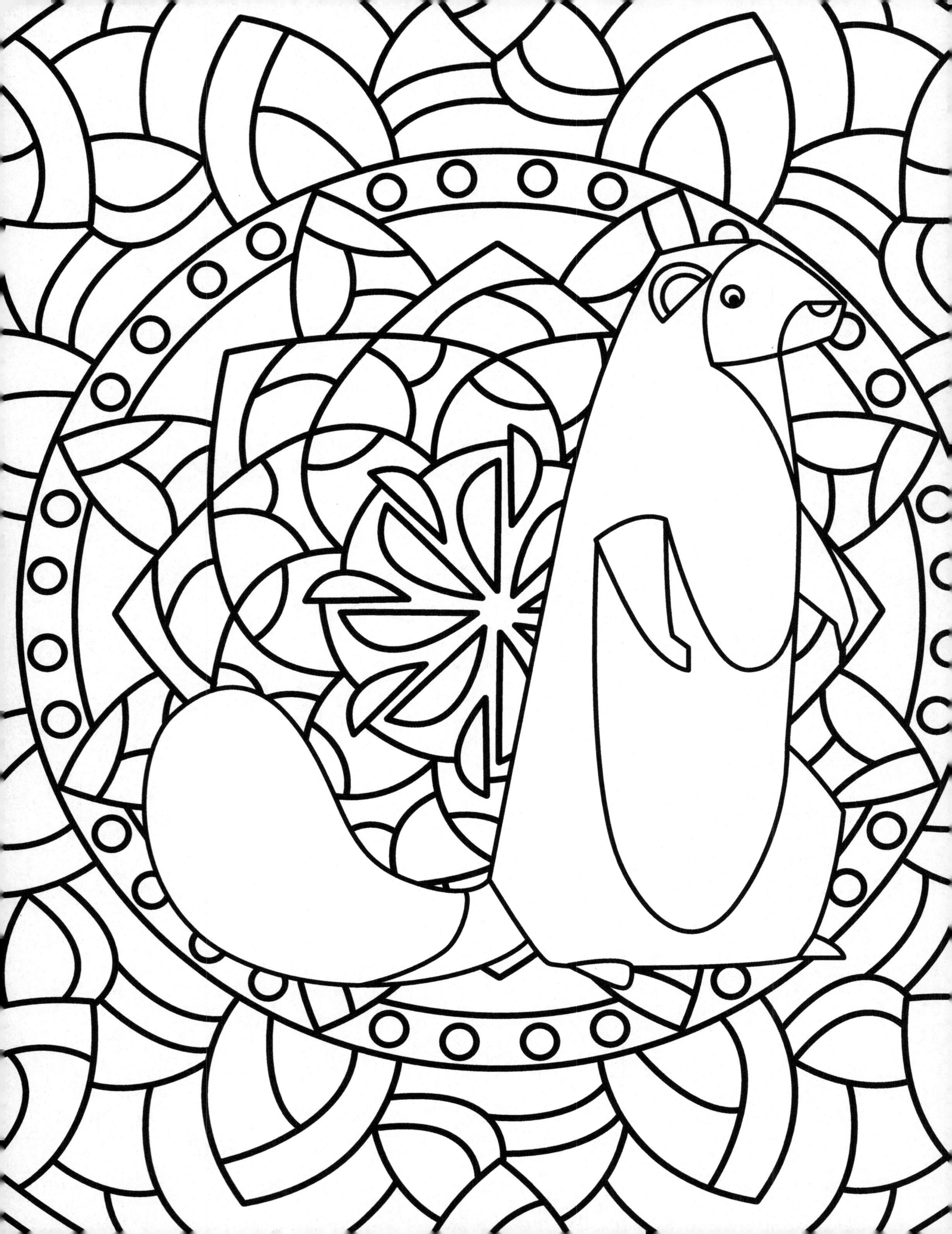

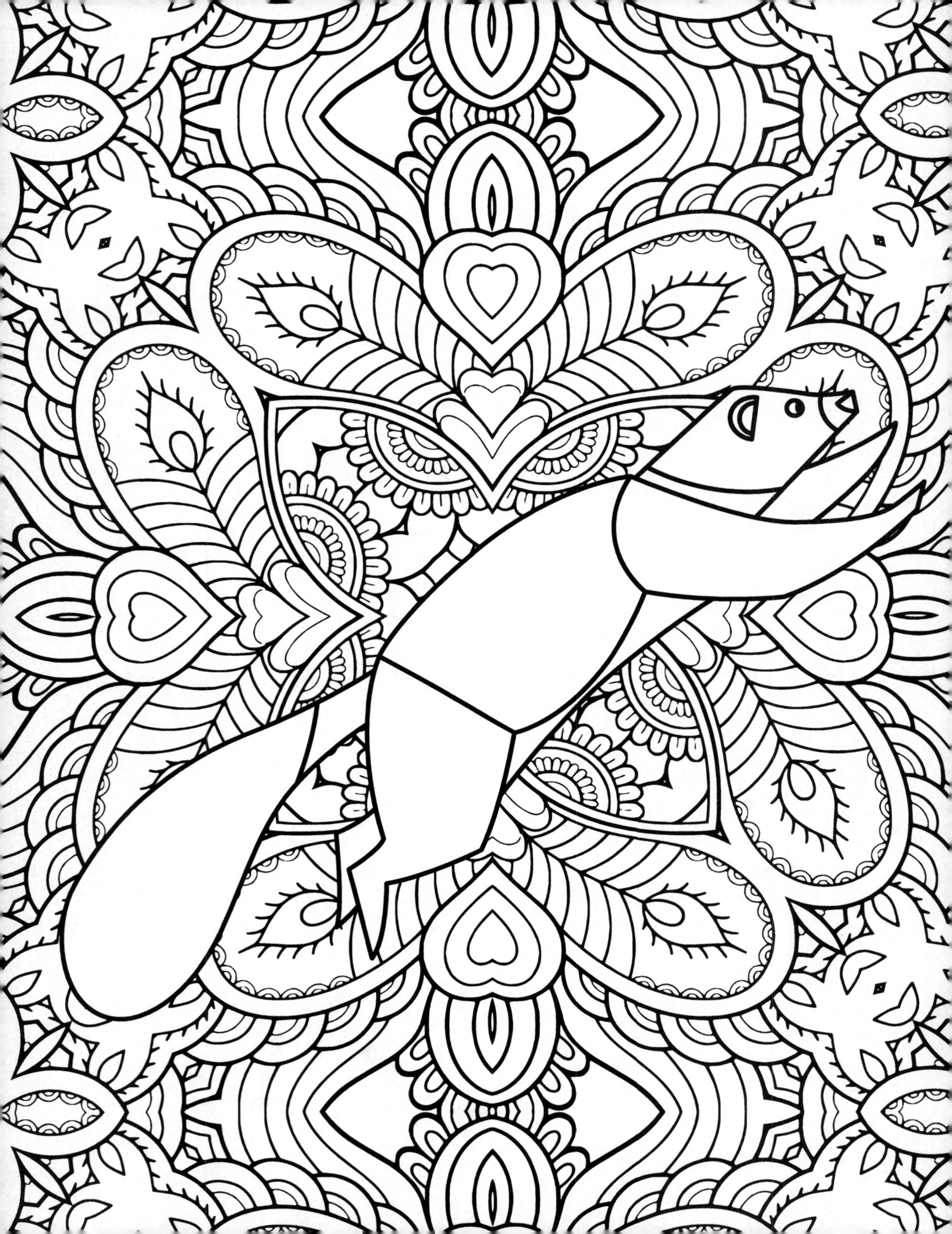

Go for it!

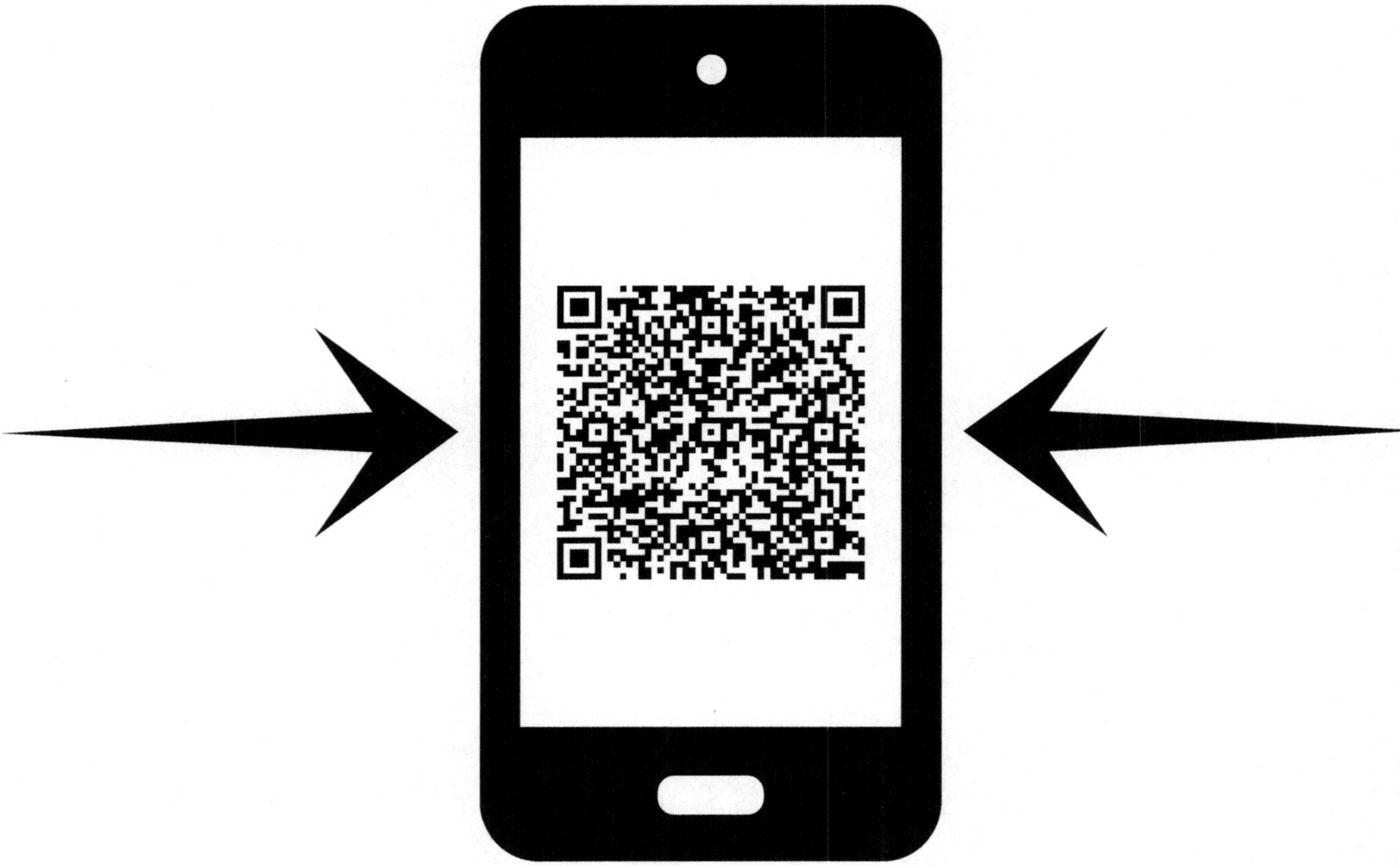